# The
# Mother
# Who
# Seeks After God

LAURA MARTIN

# The
# Mother
# Who
# Seeks After God

Daily Devotional for Busy Mums

LAURA MARTIN

CHRISTIAN
FOCUS

ISBN 1-84550-274-4
ISBN 978-1-84550-274-4

© Laura Martin

10 9 8 7 6 5 4 3 2 1

Published in 2007
by
Christian Focus Publications,
Geanies House, Fearn, Ross-shire,
IV20 1TW, Scotland, UK

www.christianfocus.com

Cover design by David Lund

Printed and bound by CPD Wales

# Contents

# For Georgia and Lucy

Thank you for making this task of motherhood so fun. Thank you for overlooking my failures, for always wanting cuddles, and for making daddy and me laugh so much.

*Georgia* – your compassionate heart and your helpful attitudes are such a joy to me.

*Lucy* – your adventurous spirit and your constant desire to laugh and be cuddled are things I treasure in my heart.

*Proverbs 3:5-6*

*Love Mummy xx*

**With special love to my dear mums**
Sally Beard
Julia Martin

**And because of Bryan**, who encouraged me to write it all down in the first place. Thank you for being my best friend, favourite preacher and precious husband.

# Introduction

We live in a world where success is measured by some key external elements: popularity, looks, the size of your bank account and the size and location of your home. I recently saw a bumper sticker that said it all: "Whoever dies with the most toys wins!"

This philosophy of external success has even made its way into parenting. I don't know about you but when I was expecting my eldest daughter, I had in my mind some key things which I thought would define my success as a parent. Things like getting the baby sleeping through the night by twelve weeks; keeping an immaculate home; showing hospitality at the drop of a hat and all the while *always* looking attractive for my husband.

As you can probably guess, I set myself up for discouragement and exhaustion. Eventually the reality that I was never going to be the superwoman mother that I had in my mind sank in. So what now? Well (it's with embarrassment that I am confessing this to you) I started to actually think about what I had been praying all through my pregnancy, "Father please help me to be a mother who seeks after You above all else."

You know they say that pregnancy depletes your brain cells and lowers your ability to think sensibly. Let me tell you that I am living proof of it! Thankfully the Lord opened my eyes to my wrong thinking and set me on track to consider exactly what a mother who seeks after Him really "looks like". She's not someone who majors on all the externals like I was – although there's nothing wrong with having secondary goals of that nature. But as I prayed and read the Scriptures I soon saw that the mother who seeks after God is a woman who seeks to honour and glorify Him in all she does – including the amazing and privileged task of motherhood.

This devotional book is the end product of my own personal study and desire to become such a woman. It's been a huge blessing in my life to have the truths of God's Word minister to my heart and mind in this way and my prayer is that you will be blessed and encouraged by it also.

So for those of you who might visit my home, you'll probably notice a bit of dust here and there, and a sad lack of home baking in the tins. In fact if you were to arrive without warning, I would probably be in my jeans and a sweater with my hair tied up and a token gesture of lipgloss on. But if you are coming so that we can chat about the Lord's high calling for mothers to seek after Him then our conversation will be rich indeed, for that is where my heart is.

So let's get started. Lay aside that duster (for now!), make a pot of tea, reach for your Bible and curl up in a chair ready to consider what it is to be a mother who seeks after God. May the Lord say of us as he once said of Mary: "[she] has chosen what is better, and it will not be taken away from her" (Luke 10:42).

# 1

# The Mother Who... Worships

*Ascribe to the LORD the glory due his name. Bring an offering and come before him: worship the LORD in the splendour of his holiness.*

1 CHRONICLES 16:29

Recently I was speaking to a friend who had just moved and was looking for a new church home. She attended one church and I asked her what she thought. She replied "The worship was great, but the preaching was so-so." I knew what she meant but it sounded like she was saying that worship is confined to that twenty minutes of singing before the sermon. Maybe that might even be the way you define worship. Many churches today are compartmentalising worship by the creation of "worship leaders", "worship services" and "worship teams". Although they might not mean to restrict worship to twenty minutes of fantastic music and singing, many people are growing up in churches thinking that way. That's a problem. A serious problem – because when people believe their worship is restricted to twenty minutes on a Sunday morning, what do the rest of their lives mean? A critical part of worship is hearing the Word of God preached and responding to it – and this is often not even considered as important in some churches.

So we see Christians who need their worship fix on Sunday mornings – with the right band, the right worship leader, the right atmosphere, the right songs ... suddenly worship is about them and not about God. Worship becomes an emotive, subjective response to stimulus provided by musicians, vocalists and the guy (or girl) who chooses the songs. Uh oh! Let's stop the worship whirlwind and look at how God actually wants to be worshipped!

God is to be worshipped:

## 1. In a manner worthy of His name.

> *"...worship the LORD in the splendour of his holiness"*
> (1 Chron. 16:29)

God is holy. That means that He is set apart from anything that is unclean, unrighteous, impure or sinful. Remember back to the book of Exodus chapter 3, when God called Moses to return to Egypt and deliver His people. God called to Moses from a burning bush. Moses took a few steps towards the bush for a closer look but God told Moses to remove his sandals because *"the place where you are standing is holy ground"* (Exod. 3:5). Moses then hid his face from God because he was afraid to look at Him. The holiness of God produced a reverent fear in Moses. If we have a wrong view of God, our worship will not be in a manner worthy of God. But the right view and a high view of God will cause us to worship in reverence and awe with fear and trembling.

## 2. In spirit and in truth.

> *"God is spirit, and his worshippers must worship in spirit and in truth"*
>
> (John 4:24)

To worship in spirit means that we are genuine in our worship. It's not just an outward gesture but a heart response to an awesome God. To worship in truth is to worship according to what Scripture demands of us and to what Scripture reveals to us about God.

## 3. With our lives.

*"Therefore, I urge you, brothers, in view of God's mercy, to offer your bodies as living sacrifices, holy and pleasing to God – this is your spiritual act of worship"*

(Rom. 12:1)

This confirms for us that worship is not just about a time of singing and praise. Of course that is one expression of worship, but true worship should flow from a life that is given to God for His glory, for His purpose, for His use, every single day of our lives. Worship is to happen in our homes, in our workplaces, in our cars, as we watch television or read a book, as we speak to one another, as we do the housework ... it's a 24/7 commitment.

The mother who seeks after God is a woman who worships minute after minute, hour after hour, day after day. So go ahead, ascribe to the Lord the glory due His name, bring an offering and come before Him; worship the Lord in the splendour of His holiness.

*Father what a privilege it is to worship You. Forgive me for the times I have placed a wrong emphasis on worship. I want to be a woman who worships You in spirit and in truth – with my very life. You are a holy God, worthy of worship all day, every day regardless of how I feel or what's happening in my life. Please help me to worship You as Your Word instructs us to. In Jesus' name, Amen.*

Verses for Further Study
- Psalm 8
- Psalm 19
- Matthew 2:1-2

QUESTIONS FOR REFLECTION
- Why do you worship God?
- How do you worship God?
- What hinders your worship?
- How can you begin/build on your family worship time so that your children understand what it is to worship God?

# 2

# The Mother Who... Disciples

*...train the younger women to love their husbands and children, to be self-controlled and pure, to be busy at home, to be kind and to be subject to their husbands, so that no-one will malign the word of God.*

TITUS 2:4-5

What are the qualifications of someone who disciples? A divinity degree? Years of experience teaching Sunday School? Someone well versed in the five points of Calvinism? Well, maybe. But picture instead a young woman in her early twenties, newly married, with a fondness for home-made fudge and a desire to encourage teenage girls in their relationship with Christ.

In fact it was this young woman who was my discipler and my mentor as a young teenager. One evening a week Janine would come and collect four or five of us teenage girls from our homes and take us back to the small flat she shared with her new husband. We would all pull up a cushion on the floor and study the Bible together, pray together, and talk about school, families and all else that fills the minds of teenage girls. And of course we would eat the fudge which Janine had often made especially for our time together.

While I must be honest and say that I can't remember much from the Bible studies, I can remember the godly example that

Janine showed by her life not only as a Christian woman but as a new wife, a working woman and a friend. And through spending this time with her I made it my goal to serve the Lord with commitment and zeal just as she did.

Janine did just what Paul is telling us all to do in those verses above. Look again at those verses. Notice it doesn't say, "train the older women in hermeneutics, exegesis, Bible exposition and the languages, so that they can train the younger women..."

Discipling might contain elements of some of these things (whether we know it or not) but the goal of discipling is to help someone grow in the Lord and in their ability to apply Biblical truth to their lives. The discipling relationship is about having someone to whom you can relate, live their life before you as an example of Christ's work in their own heart. You see how they serve their husband, their children, the church and their community. You are privy to their family life, their walk with the Lord and how they respond to various situations. They become a valuable resource of information, wisdom and experience.

I love seeing older couples in their relationships with each other and their family. I value and appreciate knowing about their personal convictions on issues of child rearing. I love hearing of families' traditions for Christmas and birthdays so I can be inspired for my own family. I couldn't learn all this in Bible school and I don't think it is something we can learn from the pastor as he preaches.

What about the specifics of what the older woman is to teach? Paul lists love, self-control, purity, homemaking, kindness and submission. They are all things which should flow from a heart transformed by the power of God, right? Well they should, but sometimes they don't. Sometimes we need a little help in these areas. Someone to be accountable to. Someone to teach us the joy of a heart transformed. Someone who by her very example inspires you to live just as Christ desires. Someone just like Janine!

Discipling should be a two-way process. Just as you should be learning from an older woman, you should also be teaching a younger woman. If you are the mother of daughters, you have your very own young women, ready to learn from their biggest influence, their precious mother! Dear mother, take the time to invest in a young woman's life – whether it be your own daughter or someone else's. If you don't do it, be sure that the world will certainly take the opportunity to. Invest your time, your experience, your love into another's life and watch for the harvest that the Lord will reap. Be a mother who invests in the Kingdom!

> *Father how I thank You for the godly women who have influenced my life. Thank You for their obedience to teach the younger women. Please help me to invest in others' lives so that they too might learn of You and Your ways. Please help me above all to invest time and energy into my children's lives. I pray that they would follow You, love You and serve You. In Jesus' name, Amen.*

## VERSES FOR FURTHER STUDY
- Proverbs 22:6
- Proverbs 13:14
- 2 Timothy 1:3-7
- Titus 2:3-10

## QUESTIONS FOR REFLECTION
- Who has had the most influence on your Christian life?
- How did they have the most influence?
- Who are you influencing in their Christian life? How are you influencing them?

- What are other ways that you could be involved in training the younger women?

# 3

# The Mother Who... Is Beautiful

*Your beauty should not come from outward adornment, such as braided hair
and the wearing of gold jewellery and fine clothes. Instead, it should be that of
your inner self, the unfading beauty of a gentle and quiet spirit,
which is of great worth in God's sight.*

1 PETER 3:3-4

Television, magazines and movies are all bombarding us with
images of what the world defines as beautiful. Women with
the perfect haircut, wardrobe, make-up and of course that all
important "perfect body" are paraded in front of us, telling us
"this is what beautiful looks like."

Even though our sensible minds tell us this is totally wrong,
our hearts can make us feel unattractive, unsuccessful and unpopular. And so we push ourselves harder to diet, exercise and
shop – sometimes at the expense of our health, our relationships and often our happiness. Now while looking attractive
for our husbands should be important to us, it should never
become a priority over our relationship with the Lord.

The Bible tells us that it is not our outer shell which God
considers beautiful. Instead it is the "unfading beauty of a gentle
and quiet spirit". Unsurprisingly this is quite a different image
from the thin, toned, tanned, manicured, confident, loud,

assertive "beautiful" women we see in the media. But that is easy "beauty". It's attainable by anyone who has the time and money to spend. The unfading beauty of a quiet and gentle spirit, however, is a different matter!

What does Peter mean by "a gentle and quiet spirit"? If we look at the context of these verses, we see that Peter is speaking about wives' submission to their husbands. The beautiful woman is one whose character is gentle, reverent, meek and humble towards her husband and towards God. What husband wouldn't want such a wife? In fact there are many verses which warn us against behaviour and character which is not in line with Peter's admonition.

Solomon writes, in the book of Proverbs, of many things which husbands find unattractive about their wives. Note that none of these verses refer to external appearances.

> "A wife of noble character is her husband's crown, but a disgraceful wife is like decay in his bones."
>
> (Prov. 12:4)

> "A quarrelsome wife is like a constant dripping."
>
> (Prov. 19:13b)

> "Better to live on a corner of the roof than share a house with a quarrelsome wife."
>
> (Prov. 21:9)

> "Better to live in a desert than with a quarrelsome and ill-tempered wife."
>
> (Prov. 21:19)

> "A quarrelsome wife is like a constant dripping on a rainy day; restraining her is like restraining the wind or grasping oil with the hand."
>
> (Prov. 27:15-16)

All of these are to do with character and attitudes of the heart. Isn't it interesting that Solomon doesn't once wish for a wife who is thin, or has naturally curly hair or a fair complexion? In fact Solomon does make this reference to a beautiful woman:

*"Like a gold ring in a pig's snout is a beautiful woman who shows no discretion"*

(Prov. 11:22).

Again character remains the most important thing.

Now obviously this is not to say that we are to just "let ourselves go" so that our husbands can't bear to look at us! Solomon also wrote the book of Song of Songs, and read what he wrote there: *"How beautiful you are, my darling! Oh, how beautiful! Your eyes are doves"* (1:15). And *"Like a lily among thorns is my darling among the maidens"* (2:2).

Wouldn't you like to hear such romantic things from your husband? Maybe even the Apostle Peter's wife enjoyed hearing such things from her dear husband. All Peter is saying is that beauty starts from within.

Perhaps you are feeling today that your inner self needs just as much if not more personal training than your outer self. Make today the day you strive to run the Christian race unhindered by things which can so easily entangle us (Heb. 12:1). Yes, certainly discipline and care for your body, after all it is the temple of the Holy Spirit and is your living sacrifice to God (Rom. 12:1). But just remember, *"Charm is deceptive, and beauty is fleeting; but a woman who fears the LORD is to be praised"* (Prov. 31:30). Let's keep our priorities in order.

*Father please forgive me for the times I have fallen into the world's "beauty trap". Those times when I give in to trying to attain the world's standard of beauty in order to fit in. Help me instead to pursue spiritual beauty first. Help me to attain*

*to that quiet and gentle spirit which is of worth in Your eyes
and the eyes of my husband. In Jesus' name, Amen.*

VERSES FOR FURTHER STUDY

- Matthew 23:27
- 1 Sam. 16:7

QUESTIONS FOR REFLECTION

- What things do you do to achieve and maintain an attractive appearance? How regularly and for how long
  do you do them?
- What things do you do to achieve and maintain "the
  unfading beauty of a gentle and quiet spirit"? How
  regularly and for how long do you do them?
- What do you need to work on to achieve the beauty we
  learn of in the Bible? How will you do this?

# 4

# The Mother Who... Comforts

*As a mother comforts her child, so will I comfort you.*
ISAIAH 66:13

Not so long ago, I had one of "those" weeks. My daughter, Georgia, caught a bug during a long haul-flight and as a result I had a number of nights of soothing a small fevered body, rocking her gently and holding her close.

There really is nothing like rocking a small child to sleep in your arms, watching and listening as the sobs turn to whimpers and finally restful sounds of sleep.

In fact as a mother there are many opportunities to offer such comfort. I think back to when Georgia became a crawling adventurer, complete with bumps and grazes, falls and skinned knees. It was hard for me to watch her because my immediate response was to stop her from doing anything which might result in her being hurt. However, I also knew that if I did that, she wouldn't learn about her environment and how to move in it. It seems that often our role as mothers is to stand back, allow a failure and then wait for those little arms to lift up for us to pick them up.

Does this remind you, as it did me, of a picture of our Lord with us? Sometimes life hurts. Perhaps not in the sense that we fall over and graze our knee, but in times of failure, grief, loss, pain, worry and distress, loneliness and depression, the hurt to our souls is acute. All too often we hear of those who in such times turn to relationships, alcohol, drugs, shopping or dieting for their comfort. While these may temporarily relieve the pain, none are a true and lasting source of comfort. After the relationship ends, who else will be there to provide comfort? After the drugs wear off, what else will provide comfort? Once the buzz of new purchases or a few lost kilos wears off, what else will provide comfort?

God says *"As a mother comforts her child, so will I comfort you"*. Dear friend, are you in need of comfort right now? Have you had a spill in life which is causing you pain? Is there a situation which pricks the very heart of your being? Turn to Him who is able to comfort you in His arms. Give over your heartache to Him in prayer and allow Him to minister to your soul through His Word. Who else could comfort you as He longs to comfort you? Don't be fooled into thinking that God is too lofty and exalted to worry about you and your problems. King David used the metaphor of God as his shepherd. David himself was a shepherd before he was promoted to King of Israel, so he knew all about the heart of a shepherd. Consider Psalm 23 which David wrote, describing the character and attributes of the Great Shepherd.

*The Lord is my shepherd, I shall not be in want.*
*He makes me lie down in green pastures,*
*He leads me beside quiet waters,*
*He restores my soul.*
*He guides me in paths of righteousness for his name's sake.*
*Even though I walk through the valley of the shadow of death,*
*I will fear no evil, for you are with me;*

*Your rod and your staff, they comfort me.*
*You prepare a table before me in the presence of my enemies.*
*You anoint my head with oil;*
*My cup overflows.*
*Surely goodness and love will follow me all the days of my life,*
*And I will dwell in the house of the LORD for ever.*

Provider, protector, restorer, comforter – just a few of the wonderful qualities of God. Can anything or anyone else provide these in the way that our Almighty, Creator, Sovereign God can? Would not the Great Shepherd who goes to great efforts to search for His lost sheep and greatly rejoices over the sheep who is found, also then take great care to love, comfort and protect His sheep?

Do you know our Heavenly Father as your Shepherd? Have you experienced His guiding, His concern and His comfort in your life? Lift up your heart to Him now in prayer and ask Him to comfort, guide and lead you as you face this new day, whether it be shadowed by grief and pain, or filled with a seemingly endless list of things to do. *"The LORD is my shepherd I shall not be in want."*

> *Heavenly Father, Shepherd, Comforter, how wonderful is Your promise to comfort us in times of pain. Father, You know the cries of my heart. Please minister to me by Your Spirit. Thank You for Your Word the Bible which is a soothing and comforting balm to my soul. In Jesus' name, Amen.*

VERSES FOR FURTHER STUDY

- Psalm 23.
  Write a list of times when you can remember the Lord shepherded you and comforted you.
- 2 Timothy 3:16

What does this verse mean when we think in terms of "God as our comforter"? Look up the dictionary definition of the word "sufficient."

## QUESTIONS FOR REFLECTION

- What are the verses in the Bible that you turn to for comfort?
- How and why do these verses comfort you?
- Are there times or circumstances when you turn to other people or other things instead of turning to God first?
- Why can these things above be a false comfort to us?

# 5

# The Mother Who... Reaps

*Let us not become weary in doing good, for at the proper time*
*we will reap a harvest if we do not give up.*
GALATIANS 6:9

You know that feeling you experience when your child finally "gets" something you have been teaching them? Like when our eldest daughter started asking for permission to get down from the dinner table. I was thrilled, excited, proud of her and, if I am honest, I felt so relieved! Relieved? Yep, because every mealtime I was constantly having to say "Georgia, please use your manners. Say 'Please may I get down from the table?'" Day after day it went, and I was beginning to feel like a stuck record!

Then one day we were sitting having lunch and a little voice said "Mummy please down table?" (not bad for not quite two years old!) I felt so surprised that I just looked at my husband and said "Honey! Did you hear that?"

But why did I feel so surprised? I knew the principle "you reap what you sow".

I guess that I was like the folk at the church in Galatia to whom the Apostle Paul wrote the above words from Galatians. I needed to be reminded and encouraged to not become weary in the task of training my daughter.

Dear friend, these words that Paul wrote are perhaps some of the most encouraging to us as mothers. Raising children is considered by God as a good (excellent or beautiful) deed. In fact, God rates it of such a high importance in a woman's life that the Apostle Paul states that widows are not to be put on the list of widows (given special ministry) *"unless she is ... well known for her good deeds, such as bringing up children ..."* (1 Tim. 5:9-10). Raising children is a high calling! It's also a hard task, a self sacrificing task and one that requires absolute, unfailing, unconditional commitment. I guess that sheds a little light on why we are sometimes weary and tempted to give up!

Let's consider Galatians 6:9 more carefully:

*Let us not become weary in doing good, for at the proper time we will reap a harvest if we do not give up.*

What are these "good deeds" we can apply to motherhood and that we should not become weary of performing? Let me start with a couple of thoughts.

1. Teaching our children to *"honour your father and mother"* (Deut. 5:16).

The Bible places a serious requirement on children to respect their parents. Listen to the consequences for children who failed to heed this command in the Old Testament law for Israel: *"If anyone curses his father or mother, he must be put to death"* (Lev. 20:9). Obviously today we live in the New Testament era but there is a general warning we can take from this verse in Leviticus. If our children do not grow to honour and respect us as the Bible commands them to do, how will they learn to honour and respect their Heavenly Father who commands it of them? We know what the eternal outcome is for the person who does not honour God. Dear mother, don't grow weary in this task!

2. Teaching our children to *"Love the LORD your God with all your heart and with all your soul and with all your strength"* (Deut. 6:5).

3. Teaching our children to hide the Word of God in their hearts.

Psalm 119:11 says *"I have hidden your word in my heart that I might not sin against you."*

If our children know the truth of the Bible, they will never have any reason to sin against God. If they choose to sin, then they will know the consequences they face. We never know when a memorised Scripture verse might "pop" into their heads and help them out of a potentially sinful or harmful situation.

4. Teaching our children to love others.

Jesus said *"A new command I give you: Love one another"* (John 13:34).

We need to teach biblical love. It's unconditional and selfless and miles away from what the world holds up as the standard of love. Their relationships will be as the Lord wills if they understand and practise biblical love.

These are just a few "good deeds" for which we mothers tend to carry the majority of responsibility in the raising of our children. They are serious and they are heavy. But they are good! Not just because our children will grow up to be nice people who contribute positively to society, these deeds are good because they have eternal significance in the lives of our children and our children's children! Let us not become weary because at the proper time we will reap a harvest in the lives of our children.

*Father, how I thank You for the awesome responsibility of raising my children. It's a task which is so varied and busy and at times hard and tiring. Thank You for helping me and giving me strength each day. Please grant me wisdom and courage to raise them to know and love You as their Lord and Saviour. Father I pray for a rich spiritual harvest in the lives of my children. In Jesus' name, Amen.*

## Verses for Further Study

- Proverbs 20:11
- Proverbs 22:6
- Proverbs 22:15
- Proverbs 23:13-14
- Proverbs 31:27-31

## Questions for Reflection

- How are you encouraged/motivated by the verse in Galatians 6:9, and with what tasks?
- Are there things which you have been weary of doing/given up on which need to be addressed? If "yes", what? How will you continue with these?
- What harvest is being reaped in your children's lives already?
- How can you avoid becoming weary/giving up on the hard tasks of motherhood?

# 6

# The Mother Who... Is Gentle

*A gentle answer turns away wrath, but a harsh word stirs up anger.*

PROVERBS 15:1

We have a cat that in many ways is still a kitten. He will still chase bits of string and pounce on leaves blowing in the wind. But underneath that cute kitten exterior is a cat with sharp claws and a particular dislike of having his tail pulled. So when my two young daughters reach out to tug on his tail as he walks past them, I need to remind them to "be gentle". Often I will take their hands and show them how to stroke him gently in order to avoid those sharp claws. Why do I do this? Because I have learnt from experience that gentleness generally means avoiding pain.

In the same way that I remind my girls to "be gentle" when they stroke the cat, Solomon, in his great wisdom, also reminds us to be gentle when we speak. Not so that we might avoid sharp claws, but a sharp tongue which stirs up anger.

What is "gentle speech"? It is when someone speaks in love, in order to calm or take the sting out of a potentially volatile situation. Or we could even use the word "defuse" or "extinguish". That is the aim to gentle speech. We read in James 1:19 that *"everyone should be quick to listen, slow to speak and slow to become angry"*. In order to be able to defuse a situation we need to be able to heed this verse.

How many of us try to multi-task when someone is speaking to us? We peel potatoes, do the ironing, tidy the room and make the beds all while our poor husband or children are trying to tell us about their day or how they are feeling about something, or maybe they might even be asking for help with something. Is this a good listening scenario? No! It is too easy in that kind of situation to be distracted and misunderstand, miss important details, and miss the point! Then we are unable to respond appropriately. What happens next? A misunderstanding occurs and mum throws back a harsh comment because "can't you see how busy I am?" Take some time over your response. I'm not talking about the "can we have carrots instead of pumpkin for dinner?" kind of discussion. I'm speaking of those situations which require wisdom and prayer in order to defuse and avert conflict. Of course there are some situations in which time to consider and pray is not available, and an immediate response is required.

I am thinking of Hannah in 1 Samuel chapter 1. When Eli the priest accused her of being drunk, Hannah didn't have time to consider and pray about her response to the dreadful accusation. However, she still responded graciously and gently, seeking to keep the peace and do what was right. It would have been easy to respond with a biting and cutting remark – had not Hannah been a woman who sought to do the Lord's will, knowing that a godly woman is gentle in her speech.

Maybe you are wondering how on earth you can be gentle of speech when you have had young children squabbling and bickering all day. Or maybe you have a toddler (or two!) whose favourite two words are "NO!" and "MINE!" And then perhaps there is your dear sweet husband who comes home from work, walks straight past the pile of laundry in the corner of the room which has not been touched all day and wants to know if his favourite shirt is ready for him to wear to the meeting he has in half an hour? Gentleness of speech perhaps may not be the first response we might have, but however impossible the task of gentle speech seems, the Bible assures us that *"I can do everything through him who gives me strength'* (Phil. 4:13). Look back to the beginning of 1 Samuel and you will see that Hannah shared her husband with his other wife, Peninnah. It would seem that Peninnah's favourite hobby was to constantly provoke Hannah about her lack of children. Hannah had many opportunities daily to practise giving a gentle response. Hannah kept close to the Lord all through that time, just as we need to.

Believe me, I know how tiring motherhood is and I know that I have at times made excuses for my harsh speech with "I'm just really tired". But I also know that tiredness does not override obedience and responsibility. There's only one thing for it friends: *"Let your gentleness be evident to all. The Lord is near"* (Phil. 4:5).

> *Father, please forgive me for the many, many times I have responded to people in a harsh and ungracious manner. I know that a godly woman is one who guards her speech and uses her words to encourage, comfort, rebuke and teach – and yet I have so often used my words to hurt. Thank You for the example of Hannah who was gentle of speech, and for the Lord Jesus who always responded out of a heart of love. Please help me to be gentle, to listen carefully and to cautiously and wisely respond in a way that honours You. In Jesus' name, Amen.*

VERSES FOR FURTHER STUDY
- 1 Samuel 1:20
- James 3:3-12

QUESTIONS FOR REFLECTION

- What hinders you from giving a gentle answer?
- In what situations do you find it hardest to give a gentle response? Why?
- What would the gentle response be for such situations?
- How can you guard your speech and give a gentle response even when you are tired or in a hurry?

# 7

# The Mother Who... Is Trusted

*Her husband has full confidence in her and lacks nothing of value.*

Proverbs 31:11

We all have affectionate names for our spouses. "Honey", "Sweetheart", maybe even "Oikodespotes" ... or maybe not! Chances are your husband doesn't write "To my darling Oiko-despotes ..." on your anniversary cards.

The Greek word Oikodespotes means "ruler or manager of the household" and the Proverbs 31 woman was just that. Her husband was probably wealthy and they would have had property, assets and servants to manage. It was very likely that he would have been a businessman away from the home for long periods of time, leaving her in the position of managing and running the household. Alongside that she also managed her own business affairs (*"She considers a field and buys it; out of her earnings she plants a vineyard."* Prov. 31:16)

It would seem that she did an excellent job of both according to verse 11: *"Her husband has full confidence in her and lacks nothing of value."*

What does this verse mean? I believe that the overriding principle of this verse is that her husband can trust her. He can trust her to manage his household while he is away; to care for their children and provide for their needs, both physical and spiritual needs; to manage and look after the servants and other household members; to care for and to be a good steward of their home, their assets and their money.

Very sadly, it would seem that such qualities today are not sought after, strived for or attained, even in some Christian homes. Phrases like "shopaholic", "shop till you drop" and "retail therapy" undermine the seriousness of biblical standards of stewardship and good management of our households and finances. In fact you have probably heard many women describe themselves, with pride, as a shopaholic. While on the outside it appears to amuse the husbands, we hear time and time again that money and spending habits are the cause of many marital problems. An unbiblical priority cannot lead to biblical love and intimacy in a marriage.

Alongside that is the influence of the feminist movement which would have us believe that homemaking and raising a family is a demeaning, belittling, unfulfilling and boring task. This can create discontentment, bitterness and resentment in women, causing them to become unwilling to fulfil their responsibilities in the marriage and in the home. This is a tragic view of what God has designed as a woman's highest calling. If women of the past had failed to be obedient to biblical standards of women's roles and motherhood, our rich Christian history may be without heroes of the faith such as Jonathan Edwards, Charles and John Wesley, and many more. Have you considered the impact you could have not only on your family but in the wider Christian family, if you also held to this high calling for a woman in the home and family?

Are you the "Oikodespotes" of your home? Does your husband have full confidence in you? If you are able to answer a loud and resounding "YES!" to those questions, then be encouraged. You follow in the footsteps of an excellent and noble woman. If "Oikodespotes" isn't a term which could be used to describe you, then why not decide right now it soon will be!

> *Father, I thank You for allowing me to be the Oikodespotes of my home. It is a big responsibility and one with many challenges which need much wisdom. Please forgive me for the times when I have neglected this important task, and even times when I have been tempted to think the way the world thinks about my role. Help me to perform the task You have given me with excellence and contentment so my husband is able to trust me and have full confidence in me, and so that you would be honoured. In Jesus' name, Amen.*

## VERSES FOR FURTHER STUDY

- Proverbs 31:10-31
- 1 Samuel 1:1-2:11
- Proverbs 14:1
- Colossians 3:17

## QUESTIONS FOR REFLECTION

- Are you the Oikodespotes of your home?
- Does your husband have full confidence and trust in all areas of your household and family management? Is there an area which you need to bring before the Lord?
- What is the impact on a family if the mother is fulfilling her God-given role with excellence?
- What is one thing you can do today to show your husband he is able to have full confidence in you as the manager of the household?

# 8

# The Mother Who... Imitates God

> Be imitators of God, therefore, as dearly loved children.
>
> EPHESIANS 5:1

The new pastor noticed from the pulpit a young boy sitting with his head bowed throughout the sermon. The boy's father was sitting next to him, his eyes were wide and unblinking, his face solemn, leading the pastor to conclude the man was convicted by the content of the sermon. After the service the pastor made his way straight to the boy and his father, concerned to be of assistance to the pair who were so obviously affected by the message. The pastor spoke first to young Jimmy. "I noticed that you were praying throughout my sermon today son. That's very commendable. Do you want to be a great missionary when you grow up?" The father coughed and squirmed in his seat, but before he could speak Jimmy replied "Oh no pastor. When I grow up I want to be able to sleep with my eyes open just like my dad does!"

We are all imitators of something or someone. Whether it's the latest fashions, the latest diet, the latest church trends or the latest parenting "experts", we all look somewhere for example, guidance and inspiration. However the Apostle Paul tells us in his letter to the Ephesians that we are to imitate God.

What does it mean to imitate God? It means that our lives are to reflect Him by following His example and seeking to lead a righteous life by His enablement. The only way we can do that is to know God through the reading and studying of His Word the Bible which reveals Him to us. From this we learn of God's character, His attributes, His purposes, His plan and His Son.

Why would we imitate God? That's easy! We are commanded to. It's not an issue of choice, it's an issue of obedience. Imitating God is training in righteous living. The Bible teaches us that Scripture, which reveals God to us, *"is useful for teaching, rebuking, correcting and training in righteousness, so that the man [and woman] of God may be thoroughly equipped for every good work"* (2 Tim. 3:16-17). God uses His Bible to change us. The more we are changed and trained in righteous living, the more closely we can inch towards imitating God.

Look at the above verses and see one outcome of being changed into the likeness of God. *"So that the man [and woman] of God may be thoroughly equipped for every good work."* Let's firstly think about good works. 1 Timothy 5:10 gives us a few examples of good works/deeds: *"...such as bringing up children, showing hospitality, washing the feet of the saints, helping those in trouble and devoting herself to all kinds of good deeds."* Did you know that God considers raising children as a good deed? So then, the story goes that in imitating God, you are being trained in righteousness and are being thoroughly equipped for *that* task. That's fantastic!

So now we have seen what it is to imitate God, and why we are to imitate God, now we will see how we can imitate Him.

Have you ever made a new year's resolution and found it impossible to keep? Many of us every New Year's Day decide that "this is the year I will ... go walking every morning, or learn a foreign language, or climb Mount Everest." Well we may as well try and climb Mount Everest because for most of us, regardless of our good intentions, our willpower is sorely lacking. That's the problem. The Bible tells us that *"... apart from me [Christ] you can do nothing"* (John 15:5b). As hard as we try to imitate God it is impossible – if we are trying to do it *apart from God.* The Apostle Paul encourages us and gives us hope with these words. *"I can do everything through him who gives me strength"* (Phil. 4:13). We need to rely on the strength of God to help us to imitate Him. We need to be asking God for His strength, for His wisdom and for His Spirit to work in our lives to rid us of all that stands in the way of becoming more like Him, replacing it with a desire to glorify Him in all that we do. We need to hide His word in our hearts and submit ourselves to it in obedience.

So we have a choice. Do we choose to follow the latest trends and fashions, the popular and proven life management plans, or even perhaps the "Agony Aunt's" advice? Or will we choose to imitate God? It may not be the most popular, trendy or politically correct choice. But it's the right choice. Dear friend, choose to be not only a mother, but a woman who imitates God.

> *Father, I confess that at times there are attitudes and behaviours in my life which are the result of imitating the world and not You. Please forgive me. Grant in me a clean heart and help me to imitate You and Your ways. Please help me to replace the sin in my life with attributes of You, which honour You. Thank You that in imitating You and striving for a righteous life, You equip me for every good work. In Jesus' name, Amen.*

Verses for Further Study
- 2 Peter 1:3, 1:5-8
- Galatians 5:16

Questions for Reflection
- What are the common parenting trends that we are encouraged to follow today?
- How do these ideas fit with the Bible's guidelines on parenting?
- What biblical principles do you commonly follow in raising your children?
- What is one specific area of your life that you need to change in order to imitate God and follow His Word?

# 9

# The Mother Who... Loves

*Jesus replied, "If anyone loves me, he will obey my teaching. My Father will love him, and we will come to him and make our home with him."*

JOHN 14:23

I love you. Three simple words – but do they have such a simple meaning? When we say "I love you" what is it that we mean? Is it "I'm fond of you"? Or "I have strong feelings of attraction for you"? Or maybe we mean "I will love you as long as you do what I want you to do." These are all common "meanings" of love. But what about biblical love? Is there a difference?

Let's take a step back and first look at how the Bible describes love. Did you know that the Greek language (the original language of the New Testament) uses different words to describe the kind of love the writer is meaning? There are two words which are most commonly used, and they are "phileo" love and "agape" love. Phileo love is used to describe a friendship kind of love. Agape love is used to describe a sacrificial love.

John 3:16 uses the word "agape" love in the well-known verse:

*"For God so **loved** the world that he gave his one and only Son, that whoever believes in him shall not perish but have eternal life."*

There is no bigger sacrifice than that described in John 3:16. This sacrificial love is again described in 1 Corinthians 13:4-8a.

> *"Love is patient, love is kind. It does not envy, it does not boast, it is not proud. It is not rude, it is not self-seeking, it is not easily angered, it keeps no records of wrongs. Love does not delight in evil but rejoices with the truth. It always protects, always trusts, always hopes, always perseveres. Love never fails."*

There really is no room for selfishness or self-promotion in that list! Imagine the impact that this kind of love would have on relationships, families and communities! What would happen to crime rates, divorce rates, abuse rates? They would dramatically reduce, because sacrificial love is not selfish, abusive, destructive or sinful. Of course this kind of love is not natural to us. However, all is not lost. God by His Spirit enables us to love this way. In fact, He not only enables us to love this way – he commands it! And so it follows that to disobey this command is to sin.

Think about your loved ones. How do you love them? Motherhood is absolutely about sacrifice but at times perhaps this love seems like *too much* of a sacrifice. Look back at 1 Corinthians 13:4-8a. This would tell us that our love to our husband and children must be shown by our patience, kindness, forgiveness, calmness, humility and so on. Are there times that it seems too hard to display all of these qualities in your life? Maybe you have not had a full night's sleep since before you started having children, you are exhausted and survival is your primary aim. Maybe you feel that if you can just get through the day and get the kids fed, bathed and in bed without having to worry about anything or anyone else, then you have done well. Anything else on top of that is too hard. Think on this.

Do you think that the Lord Jesus saw the task ahead of Him as particularly easy? Of course He didn't – in fact He sweated drops of blood just thinking about it. But He went ahead with it anyway. He allowed Himself to be nailed to a cross, to be mocked and taunted, to have every ounce of dignity literally stripped away from Him. Why did He do it? Because He sacrificially loves us. That is love. And that is the example that we are to follow.

Jesus said, *"If anyone loves me, He will obey my teaching"* (John 14:23a).

Do you love Jesus? And if you do, how do you love Him? In the way that the world loves or with a sacrificial kind of love – such as the love that Jesus has for you and for me?

*Father, thank You for loving me so much that You gave Your one and only Son, that I might not perish but instead have eternal life. There is no greater love than that. Please help me to obey You, by loving others sacrificially. I know that I cannot do this by myself and I thank You for Your Spirit who helps me and strengthens me for the task. Be glorified in me I pray. In Jesus' name, Amen.*

VERSES FOR FURTHER STUDY
- 1 Corinthians 13:1-3
- Matthew 22:37
- Titus 2:4

QUESTIONS FOR REFLECTION
- Prior to reading this devotion today, how would you have defined love? Is it any different to biblical love?
- How do you show love to others?
- What do you expect from those who love you?
- How do your above answers measure up against 1 Corinthians 13:4-8a?

- What sacrifices have you made for your family? For God?
- Will the way that you show love to your family/ to God look any different now? If so, how?

# 10

# The Mother Who... Is Praised

> "Many women do noble things, but you surpass them all".
> Charm is deceptive, and beauty is fleeting; but a woman who fears the LORD
> is to be praised. Give her the reward she has earned, and
> let her works bring her praise at the city gate.
> PROVERBS 31:29-31

Have you ever read Proverbs 31:10-31 and felt just a little discouraged? I mean, here is this amazing woman who can turn her hand to anything from dressmaking and catering to entrepreneurial business and property investment, and all of it is done with excellence! There is no clue that anything she ever did was left unfinished or done poorly. Neither is there any sign of burnout, overload or nervous anxiety! And what does the husband of such a woman do? He praises her – and so he should!

In today's society, this woman would be held up as the woman who has it all. She has a wonderful home life, two satisfying careers (not just property investment but foreign trading as well!), and to top it off, a wonderful relationship with her children, and a husband who praises her.

Yep, that's a little discouraging from my perspective. Some days it's all I can do to keep on top of the laundry, the house clean, meals on the table and maybe grow a few vegetables in the garden! If I achieve much more than that in a day then I can't wait till dinner time so I can tell my husband my "great achievement" and so receive a pat on the back! But wait a second – what is the Lord actually praising our Proverbs 31 friend for? Read through those verses again and you will see that it's not her "doing" that He is praising. It's her relationship with Him. In fact, God says that it is a woman who *fears the Lord* who is to be praised. Not the woman who is the perfect homemaker, but the woman who "*fears the Lord*". Everything else we **do** will be an outflow of a heart that fears the Lord because we want to honour Him and serve Him with excellence.

You see, nothing else really falls into place until your relationship with the Lord is right. You can have the cleanest home in the street, the most polite children, your husband's favourite meals on the table every night – and yet if your relationship with the Lord is not as it should be, your service to Him and to your family is marred.

How do we know if our lives reflect the fear of the Lord? Well, let's look at the life of the Proverbs 31 woman and see what we can learn from her.

1. She submits to and serves her husband (vv. 11-12)
2. She sacrificially serves her family (v. 15)
3. She sacrificially serves others (vv. 15-20)
4. She is generous and charitable (v. 20)
5. She is diligent and hard-working (vv. 13-20, 22, 27)
6. She is a good steward of the resources she has (v. 16)
7. She enables her husband to achieve his calling (v. 23)
8. She is not anxious, instead she trusts the Lord (v. 25)
9. She speaks with wisdom (v. 26)
10. She is not lazy (v. 27)
11. Others see her obedience to the Lord (vv. 23, 28-31)

There are a lot of qualities here which exemplify a life which fears the Lord. Take some time to evaluate your own life. Think about all that you do which befits a woman who fears the Lord. Consider your devotional life, your actions, your words and your thought life.

We learn from the Proverbs 31 woman that our life should be one of respect, service, love, obedience and sacrifice to the Lord. In this world we are praised for our looks, our careers, the size of our home and our bank account. Let's not seek after the praise of man, but instead let's strive daily to seek after the praise of God.

*Father, thank You for Your Word which teaches us what is truly worthy of praise. Help me not to be a woman who seeks after the praise of man but instead longs for praise from You. Please, with the help of Your Spirit, enable me to honestly evaluate my life before You so that I might turn away from all that is not praiseworthy in Your sight.*

*In Jesus' name, Amen.*

VERSES FOR FURTHER STUDY

- Proverbs 31:10-31
- Proverbs 27:2
- Proverbs 25:27

QUESTIONS FOR REFLECTION

- Whose praise do you seek after? The praise of man (your family, friends, husband, pastor) or the praise of God?
- Could your family say Proverbs 31:30 about you?
- List the qualities in your own life which reflect a woman who fears the Lord.
- List the qualities in your own life which do not reflect a woman who fears the Lord. What things do you need to address?

# 11

# The Mother Who... Presses On

*But one thing I do: Forgetting what is behind and straining towards what is ahead, I press on towards the goal to win the prize for which God has called me heavenwards in Christ Jesus.*

PHILIPPIANS 3:13-14

"Don't look back." This is what one of the angels who was about to destroy Sodom told Lot and his family as they were fleeing the city. "Don't look back."

Why do you think the angel gave that instruction? Perhaps it was because he wanted to spare them seeing their city, their home and possibly their friends, being obliterated. Or maybe he didn't want them to be distracted from reaching their goal of getting back to a safe place. Or maybe it was even a test of their obedience. Perhaps it was none of these; the Bible doesn't actually tell us. But regardless of the reason, there was a very tragic consequence to pay for looking back.

Lot's wife looked back, and as we read in Genesis 19:26 she was turned into a pillar of salt. She lost her life. Her husband became a widower, and her daughters lost their mother. Absolute tragedy to a family – all because she did not heed the advice – "Don't look back."

Why did Lot's wife look back? It had to be more than mere curiosity. Some Bible teachers would suggest that she didn't really want to leave the city she loved – that her heart longed to return to Sodom. What a shocking thing, to think that Abraham's niece-in-law would rather have lived in a city where God pronounced the sin of the people so unrighteous that the only option left for Him was to destroy the city and all its inhabitants; and for that, she also was destroyed.

There are many reasons why we, in our own Christian walk, might be tempted to look back. Our hearts hide regrets, longings, thoughts of "if only", or "what if", or maybe even "why me?" Sometimes we long to return to easier times, happier times, more prosperous times. But the Apostle Paul knew that looking back was of no benefit to us. He knew that we could not move ahead in the life that the Lord has given us to live if we are constantly looking back to the past.

Observe what Paul writes in Philippians 3:4-11. Paul is talking of his past life, so to speak, as a Pharisee. In the eyes of man, Paul had it all going for him. He followed the Law to the rule; he gave himself completely and zealously to fulfilling his role of Pharisee. However, he then goes on to say *"But whatever was to my profit I now consider loss for the sake of Christ"* (v. 7). Read on to verses 10-11 to find out why he had this attitude. *"I want to know Christ and the power of his resurrection and the fellowship of sharing in his sufferings, becoming like him in his death, and so, somehow, to attain to the resurrection from the dead."*

That was what Paul was straining for and reaching towards. His goal was to become more and more like Christ. He knew that the life he had left was nothing compared to knowing Christ.

That is to be the attitude of us all. We should all be pressing on to become more like Christ. However, there is much along the way that can distract us from this. Perhaps you might have feelings of dissatisfaction with "your lot". Even though you would not give up your children for the world, maybe there are at times a desire to return to "the good old days". Those days when you had more time for you, more money in the bank, more time alone with your husband, more sleep, more, more, more – for you! If we give in to thinking these things, what happens in our hearts? Our desire for Christ is replaced by a desire for "me". We feel sorry for ourselves, bitterness creeps in, and it eats away at us and becomes the motive for everything we do or say.

Paul tells us in 2 Corinthians how to deal with that wrong thinking. *"...take captive every thought to make it obedient to Christ"* (2 Cor. 10:5).

Take captive every wrong thought, repent from it and then forget about it – and press on, without looking back, to become more like Christ.

What keeps you from pressing on towards the ultimate goal? What distracts you from moving ahead? Commit each distraction to the Lord and press on in faith. And remember, "Don't look back."

*Father, thank you for Paul's words of encouragement to "press on" to our goal of becoming more like Jesus. As we consider Lot's wife we are reminded of the tragic consequences of a heart that is not focused on You. Please help me to forget all that is behind me and to keep my eyes focused on You. Forgive me for the times I have looked back, becoming distracted and maybe even falling behind instead of moving ahead. Help me to be a mother who presses on towards the goal of knowing Christ and becoming more like Him. In Jesus' name, Amen.*

VERSES FOR FURTHER STUDY
- Genesis 19:1-29
- Philippians 3:4b-15
- Hebrews 12:1

QUESTIONS FOR REFLECTION
- What "things" do you need to forget in order to press on?
- How can you make this a daily practice to ensure you "don't look back"?
- Who else in the Bible are good examples of those who "press on"?
- What can you learn from them?

# 12

# The Mother Who... Teaches

*I will instruct you and teach you in the way you should go.*
PSALM 32:8

You've heard the saying "The hand that rocks the cradle rules the world." Here's another one: "Behind every successful man lies an equally successful woman – his mother!"

Although these may be just written in jest, they perhaps do speak some truth.

As mothers, we have the great responsibility of teaching our children about the Lord. There are two women who come to my mind when I think on this awesome task. In fact these two women are given only a very brief mention, but they are so significant. Any ideas who? I am referring to Eunice and Lois, the mother and grandmother of Timothy.

Timothy was a young pastor, on his own in his first pastorate. His mentor, teacher and friend, the Apostle Paul, wrote 1 and 2 Timothy (often referred to as the Pastoral Epistles) to encourage Timothy in his life and his ministry. In 2 Timothy, Paul makes mention of Timothy's mother and grandmother in a familial way. *"I have been reminded of your sincere faith, which first lived in your grandmother Lois and in your mother Eunice and, I am persuaded, now lives in you also"* (2 Tim. 1:5).

Eunice and Lois were obedient to the Lord in training Timothy in the knowledge and ways of God. It would seem that because of their obedience, Timothy was led to saving faith and went on to serve the Lord in a mighty way. What would have happened if they had not been obedient?

Another mother obedient to the call of training and teaching her children was the mother of King Lemuel. Again we hear nothing else of this woman – not even her name – but we see evidence of her faithful teaching to her adult son who was a King! Curious? Take a look at Proverbs 31.

There are many more women throughout history who have been faithful to the command to *"train a child in the way he should go, and when he is old he will not turn from it"* (Prov. 22:6). Two well-known mothers are Sarah Edwards and Susannah Wesley. Both of these women reared children who played a significant part in the church and also in the world.

Of course we cannot guarantee that our obedience in teaching our children will result in their salvation. That is in God's sovereign hands and for that we must be thankful.

So, how do we train our children in the ways of the Lord? Deuteronomy 6:6-9 says *"These commandments that I give you today are to be upon your hearts. Impress them on your children. Talk about them when you sit at home and when you walk along the road, when you lie down and when you get up. Tie them as symbols on your hands and bind them on your foreheads. Write them on the door-frames of your houses and on your gates."*

Here are a few basic principles from these verses.

1. Your relationship with the Lord must be genuine and real.

*"Let the word of Christ dwell in you richly as you teach and admonish one another with all wisdom, and as you sing psalms, hymns and spiritual songs with gratitude in your hearts to God."*

(Col. 3:16)

2. Use everyday activities to teach your children from the Bible and about the Lord.

3. Ensure your lifestyle reflects godly living.

4. Make your home a place that reflects the home of a family who serves God.

Many parents today are happy for their children to attend Sunday School for their spiritual input, in the same way that their own spiritual input comes only from Sunday sermons. These verses in Deuteronomy speak of a relationship with God which goes beyond Sundays. It is a part of every activity, every day.

Your faithfulness and obedience just might cause you to see a "Timothy", or a "Charles or John Wesley" emerge from your family.

*Father, thank You for the precious gift of (your child/ren's names). With all my heart I long for them to receive You as their Saviour and Lord. Please teach me from Your Word that I might also teach my children of You. By Your Spirit I would ask that You do a transforming work in their hearts. In Jesus' name, Amen.*

VERSES FOR FURTHER STUDY
- Deuteronomy 4:9
- Luke 11:1-2
- Proverbs 1:8
- 2 Timothy 3:16

QUESTIONS FOR REFLECTION

- What is one specific activity that you do with your children which could be used to teach them of God and His character?
- What can be done in your home to make sure it reflects a family who worships God?
- What can you specifically pray for your children as you teach them and train them?

# 13

# The Mother Who... Grows in the Lord

*Like newborn babies, crave pure spiritual milk,*
*so that by it you may grow up in your salvation.*
1 PETER 2:2

I remember being out shopping when my eldest daughter, (then just a few weeks old) reminded me very loudly that it was her mealtime. I couldn't find a mother-and-baby room and for the twenty minutes that it took me to find one, Georgia's screams got louder and louder. I tried everything I could think of to distract her. I cuddled her, sang to her, I even gave her my finger to suck on ... but to no avail. She knew just what she wanted! When we finally found the room I began to feed her and ... silence. Her hunger was satisfied.

That is just the intensity that the Apostle Peter is speaking of when he says *"like newborn babies, crave pure spiritual milk"*. But what does he really mean by it?

In the verses prior to this command, Peter reminds the Christians of the work that God has done in their lives. He tells them to rid themselves of things which should not be present in the life of one who has received Christ. Then he moves on to encouraging them to grow spiritually – by craving pure spiritual milk. Peter is speaking here of God's Word the Bible. There is no other way to grow in our relationship with God apart from filling our minds and hearts with His Word.

Sadly there are many churches today that no longer stand for this truth. They have been misguided by false teachers who say that the Bible is not important and they focus primarily on seeking some kind of experience of God. The problem with this is that, aside from the fact that it is unbiblical, it is also potentially dangerous because people end up riding "the emotional roller coaster of faith". If they feel great and everything is going their way, then they can say that God is great. If they are not feeling great, they start to doubt God, deny His sovereignty and they hold His promises in contempt. Their faith has no sure footing and their view of God and their feelings towards God are literally all over the place. Why do these folk believe this false teaching? Because they don't know and understand God's Word for themselves, and as a result they are vulnerable to popular thinking that comes along.

Jesus warns us of such false teachers in Matthew 7:15, *"Watch out for false prophets. They come to you in sheep's clothing, but inwardly they are ferocious wolves"*.

Those who are "babies" in the faith are not mature enough to know false teaching. That's why Peter tells us that just as newborn babies crave milk – which is the only thing that nourishes them and helps them to grow – Christians should feed only on that which will nourish and help them grow.

The Apostle Paul's words to his young friend Timothy assures us that God's Word is all we need to grow and mature us in our Christian walk. *"All Scripture is God-breathed and is useful for teaching, rebuking, correcting and training in righteousness so that the man of God may be thoroughly equipped for every good work"* (2 Tim. 3:16-17).

That is exactly what spiritual growth is, right? It's becoming righteous. For in growing righteous, we are growing more like the Lord, therefore glorifying Him.

There are so many wonderful resources which will assist us in our spiritual growth. The Bible has to be the first and foremost "nourishment" in our "spiritual diet", but there are many other wonderful resources which are like our spiritual dessert! Things such as study notes, commentaries, online sermons, books, conferences – what blessings we can enjoy!

So – how is your spiritual diet looking? Are there things you crave or feed on instead of the Word of God? The world's influence can be so subtle in diverting our hunger for the Word towards cravings for material possessions, money, relationships, looks and so on.

Be the mother who grows in the Lord by feeding daily on His Word.

*Father, thank You for Your Word which is sufficient for all that we need to live a godly life. Thank You that Your Word is powerful and changes lives. Please transform my heart and cause me to hunger intensely after Your Word. May nothing else satisfy that hunger so I might grow to be more like You each day. In Jesus' name, Amen.*

## VERSES FOR FURTHER STUDY

- 2 Timothy 3: 1-5
- 2 Peter 3:18

## QUESTIONS FOR REFLECTION

- What is the content of your spiritual diet?
- Can you look back over the last twelve months and see areas of growth in your Christian life?
- What areas of your Christian life would you like to grow in over the next twelve months?

# 14

# The Mother Who... Is Holy

*But just as he who called you is holy, so be holy in all you do;*
*for it is written "Be holy, because I am holy"*
1 PETER 1:15-16

How would you define holy? Some time ago I read the above verse and wondered what it would "look like" to be holy and living a holy life. The first things which came to mind were images of serene living, pure living and loveliness. I thought of holiness as something which is untouched by the grime of sin and is instead something to be drawn to.

Then I started thinking of how these images compared to the reality of my life. Life which at that time consisted of early-morning and late-evening battles with rush-hour traffic, working in a health system overloaded by patients and sorely lacking in funding. Once I made it home it was a rush to prepare dinner so that we could be out the door to a meeting of some sort, only to return home late and drop into bed exhausted and dreading another day the same! The more I thought about how ugly and chaotic my days seemed, the more discouraged I felt – until that is, I remembered the life the Lord lived while on earth. His was a holy life that was grieved daily by the effects of the Fall. He faced legalistic Pharisees, sickness, poverty, hardened and unrepentant hearts, and betrayal by one who was supposedly a follower. He even came face to face with Satan. But still He remained holy, set apart. That's what holy means: set apart from sin to God.

I look at that and I think "Wow! I could never be like that." But there is a problem with that thinking. I have to be like that. The Bible demands it of us.

Hebrews 12:14 says, *"Make every effort to live in peace with all men and to be holy; without holiness no-one will see the Lord."*

We cannot witness saving faith to others if we ourselves are not holy. If we know that to be holy means that we are to be set apart, then the question is, how are we to achieve that?

The Apostle Paul writes to the church at Rome of this very topic.

> *"I put this in human terms because you are weak in your natural selves. Just as you used to offer the parts of your body in slavery to impurity and to ever-increasing wickedness, so now offer them in slavery to righteousness leading to holiness. When you were slaves to sin, you were free from the control of righteousness ... But now that you have been set free from sin and have become slaves to God, the benefit you reap leads to holiness, and the result is eternal life"* (Rom. 6:19-20, 22).

So there is our answer. We are set apart by righteous living which leads to holiness. Righteous lives lived the way that Jesus lived His life here on earth. Let's take a quick look at three of Jesus' "holy qualities".

1. Love.

Jesus is known for loving those who were difficult to love (that includes you and me). Look at how He loved His chosen people: *"O Jerusalem, Jerusalem ... how often I have longed to gather your children together, as a hen gathers her chicks under her wings, but you were not willing!"* (Luke 13:34).

2. Forgiveness.

Jesus demonstrated His holy forgiveness even as He was nailed to the cross. *"Father, forgive them, for they do not know what they are doing"* (Luke 23:34).

3. Obedience.

Even Jesus struggled with the task He came to earth to fulfil. Luke 22:42 tells us how Jesus prayed to His Father that He might be removed from the dreadful situation ahead. But God did not remove Him – so He obeyed even unto death.

In just these three qualities, Jesus demonstrates to us holy living. In each of these three qualities He is set apart from the world. He is different.

I wrote the following poem with all these things in mind.

What does it mean to be holy?
White robes, a mournful face?
A stool on a cloud with a harp on your knee?
No! It means be in the world – but not of it!
Your thought life filtered through the Word,
Your actions guided by the Spirit,
Your hope on the promise of eternity with Him.
Be holy for I am holy,
Not just a command for obedience
But a response out of thankfulness
For the gift of God –
Eternal life
In Jesus.

*Father, I want to be like You. Please forgive me for the many times that my life is not holy and set apart for You. Please help me to live in righteousness and seek after You in all things. May others see You in me. In Jesus' name, Amen.*

## VERSES FOR FURTHER STUDY

- 2 Corinthians 6:16-7:1
- Ephesians 4:17-24

## QUESTIONS FOR REFLECTION

- What other qualities of Jesus' life demonstrate holy living?
- How can you be holy in your family, community and neighbourhood?
- How can you teach your family what it means to live a holy life?
- How can you better strive to live a holy life?

# 15

# The Mother Who... Laughs

*She is clothed with strength and dignity; she can laugh at the days to come.*

PROVERBS 31:25

What makes you laugh? Perhaps a good joke or a crazy situation might make you laugh. Or maybe you know one of those people who can make even the dullest tasks and situations hilarious. But I wonder if thinking of the days to come makes you laugh?

Even though I would not say that I am a pessimist, there are times when I think about the future and the possible loss of family members, possible financial struggles, and I wonder whether my children will come to know the Lord as their Saviour. These are situations that cause my stomach to tangle in knots when I think about them. Hardly laughing matters!

But this virtuous Proverbs 31 woman certainly does laugh. Not because she is anticipating an amusing future, and not because she has finally gone crazy from all those early mornings, busy days and late nights. No, she laughs because she is *"clothed with strength and dignity"*. She has chosen to clothe her heart and her mind not with worry and anxiety, but with godly qualities of strength and dignity. And these qualities not only enable her to trust in the Lord's plan for the future, they also enable her to rejoice in it!

That sounds great, doesn't it? But how exactly do we clothe ourselves with these qualities? Is there some magic pill we can take? Or maybe some catchy and cute little phrase we can repeat over and over when times get tough? Afraid not. These "godly clothes" are all about choice. We must choose to put them on each day. Let's take a look at the wondrous outfit we must wear, the outfit otherwise known as "the armour of God".

> *"For our struggle is not against flesh and blood, but against the rulers, against the authorities, against the powers of this dark world and against the spiritual forces of evil in the heavenly realms. Therefore put on the full armour of God ... Stand firm then, with the belt of truth buckled round your waist, with the breastplate of righteousness in place, and with your feet fitted with the readiness that comes from the gospel of peace ... take up the shield of faith, with which you can extinguish all the flaming arrows of the evil one. Take the helmet of salvation and the sword of the Spirit which is the word of God"* (Eph. 6:12-17).

So there we have it. Six pieces of spiritual armour with which to face the daily spiritual battle that seeks to discourage, worry and destroy us.

Rely upon the power of God and set yourself firmly in the Truth, ridding yourself of anything which hinders your Christian walk. Live in righteousness and obedience. Stand firm in the knowledge that you are, through the gospel, at peace with God and trust in God to help you and protect you as you face temptations, doubts and trials. Be encouraged in the knowledge and assurance of God's faithfulness to accomplish your full salvation and *know* God's Word so you can use it when Satan attacks you with his fiery darts.

What a fantastic outfit to wear! To be clothed in such a way readies us for action, and comforts us as we face the unknown situation of "tomorrow". No wonder the Proverbs 31 woman could laugh at the future. She has all she needs to face it. And, for that matter, so do we. Now that's something to smile about!

> *Father, please forgive my worrying heart. I know that You are the Almighty and Sovereign God and that You are also my Father who cares for every detail of my life. Thank You for promising to give me all that I need to cope with every minute of every day. Help me to daily put on the armour of God. In Jesus' name, Amen.*

VERSES FOR FURTHER STUDY
- Isaiah 40:28-31
- Isaiah 41:10
- Psalm 84:5

QUESTIONS FOR REFLECTION
- How do you respond when you think of "tomorrow"?
- How can you practically put on the full armour of God every day?
- How has God strengthened you, encouraged you, protected you and carried you through difficult times in the past?
- Why can you, like the Proverbs 31 woman, laugh at days to come?

# 16

# The Mother Who... Perseveres

*Consider it pure joy, my brothers, whenever you face trials of many kinds,
because you know that the testing of your faith develops perseverance.
Perseverance must finish its work so that you may be
mature and complete, not lacking anything.*

JAMES 1:2-4

A while ago, I was listening to my favourite preacher (my husband of course) when he spoke of this word "perseverance". He said that the Greek word means to "remain under" (the trial). To the rational person this probably sounds absurd. Who doesn't want to look for better, easier or more comfortable options when the going gets tough? In fact, even when the going isn't tough we still look for the easiest options – microwave food, remote controls, wireless connection ... anything to make life a little easier.

Unfortunately this "easiest option" philosophy has muscled its way into perhaps inappropriate areas of our lives. Finding that university course too difficult? Just drop out till something easier comes along. Can't seem to save enough for that big family holiday you've always wanted? Just get a loan and pay it back later. Struggling to find time for your quiet times each day? Just console yourself with the thought of getting back into them when the children are older or the workload is less or the days have more hours in them.

The problem in doing so is that when we truly do strike a trial we are not equipped with the skill of perseverance in order to get us through it. However, I have learnt that perseverance is a skill that God calls us to use quite regularly. Let's learn why.

Look back at today's verse. Do you see something interesting there? James makes a direct connection of a trial being used to test our faith. Trials are not random acts or occurrences – they have a purpose. Every trial we face tests our faith and then develops in us perseverance if we respond the right way. And what does it say next? *"Perseverance must finish its work so that you may be mature and complete, not lacking anything"* What does that mean? It means that through our persevering, God is helping us to grow more like Christ. It's called sanctification.

Think of Jesus who, while on the earth, persevered in all situations regardless of the fact that at any time He could call on hosts of angels to minister to Him, protect Him and fight for Him. I think particularly of how He persevered with His disciples. Twelve men from various backgrounds, none with any notable outstanding gifts or achievements. For three years Jesus trained them in His ways and taught them truth. Why? So that when He returned to heaven, they would fulfil the great commission: *"Therefore go and make disciples of all nations, baptising them in the name of the Father and of the Son and of the Holy Spirit, and teaching them to obey everything I have commanded you"* (Matt. 28:19-20).

What were the results of such training? They were fearful of being in a storm even though the One who created and controlled the elements was with them in the flesh (Mark 4:35-39). They did not have hearts of shepherds caring for the flock and instead wanted to call down fire from heaven on those who did not receive Jesus (Luke 9:51-56). After three years one betrayed Him, handing Him over to those who wanted to kill Him (John 18:2-5). One denied Him to protect his own life (John 18:15-18). One doubted Him (John 20:24-29).

Now if you or I had the task of selecting those who were to go out and be missionaries to the world, we probably would have given up on these guys after the first week of training! But Jesus didn't. He demonstrated the ultimate example in perseverance. Why? Not because He needed to persevere in order to grow in spiritual maturity. He did it to be an example for us to follow. If your heart is sinking as you are thinking about the task He is asking you to face right now then be encouraged. He has also promised that we can do all things through Him (Phil. 4:13).

As Christians we should expect to often be in situations which require us to persevere. Don't look for an easy option out, for it is through perseverance that you will grow to be more like Christ. And after all, isn't that what we are aiming at?

*Oh Father how I wish that I was able to easily persevere through trials and hard situations. It is so hard, especially when I can see that there might be an easier option or even a way out. Please forgive me and help me to remember that You have promised that I can do all things through You. Help me to grow more like Jesus I pray. In Jesus' name, Amen.*

## VERSES FOR FURTHER STUDY
- Philippians 3:12-14
- Hebrews 12:1-13
- James 1:1-12
- 1 Peter 1:6-7

QUESTIONS FOR REFLECTION

- What qualities and behaviours should we display through a trial?

- Think back to a recent trial. What qualities and behaviours did you display? Does your list compare with question one? Is there any way you could have responded more biblically to your trial?

- How can you tell someone who is persevering under a trial, as opposed to someone who is putting up with it because they have no choice?

- How can you encourage your family to persevere under a trial?

# 17

# The Mother Who... Submits

*"I am the Lord's servant,"* Mary answered. *"May it be to me as you have said."*
<br>Luke 1:38

Out of the many godly women and men in the Bible who lived their lives in submission for the Lord, this account of Mary is one that really touches my heart and stirs my own convictions.

Let's set the scene. A young Mary was engaged to be married to Joseph, a local carpenter. There's nothing unusual about that until, that is, Mary receives a visit from an angel. While that in itself is something quite mind-boggling, the purpose of the angel's visit is to tell Mary that she will give birth to the Son of God. Suddenly her world is turned upside down. Mary knows instantly that not only is her proposed marriage at risk, but her life is on the line also. She knows that her own family and probably even her own fiancé will have a hard time believing her story about a visit from an angel and a divinely planned pregnancy. People are sure to assume that she has committed adultery, and for that she could be shunned by her family and community and maybe even put to death. Her dream of becoming a wife and mother, of managing her home, shattered in an instant.

What was Mary's response to all of this? Pure and instant submission. Pure because she had nothing to gain and everything to lose. She placed herself completely under the authority of God in this difficult situation. And she did it instantly – not after she had thrown a tantrum and then had time to think about it and get over it. Not even after she had time to pray about it. Instant submission.

Often we think about submission in terms of marriage. We read books and do Bible studies on this role of the wife, but first we need to understand that submission in marriage as God requires it is really just an overflow of our submission to Him.

There are many people today who would have us believe that being a Christian is all about us. It's about God being our friend, Him meeting our needs, Him making us healthy, wealthy and successful. This comes from having a wrong and incomplete view of God. Yes God is loving and kind, patient and compassionate, our provider and our friend. But it is also equally true that He is a just and holy God, a jealous God, a God who seeks first place in our lives. This is the God to whom Mary submitted. He is the same God today as He was yesterday, and He will be the same tomorrow as well. The submission He required from Mary is the same that He requires from us.

The Lord Jesus showed this same submission to His Father. From His example we see that at times, submission is a very difficult task. Jesus shows us in Luke 22:42-44 just how to deal with that difficulty. It is the account of the Lord very soon to face His death. He earnestly prayed to His Father to remove Him from that situation. But then He followed that up by saying *"yet not my will, but yours be done."* What happened then? Did He instantly feel better about it? No – but an angel of the Lord appeared to Him and strengthened Him. Even after the angel had appeared, Jesus continued to anguish over the situation. So He continued to pray. Submission is tough and at times demands from us more than we feel that we can give. God knows that and ministers to us by His Spirit, through His Word and through prayer.

Are you facing tough times in which you need to submit yourself to the Lord? Maybe illness, financial pressures, marital difficulties? Let's learn from Mary two attitudes which are essential if we are to willingly submit to the Lord in these times.

1. Mary accepted that first of all she was a servant of God. Not a pal or a friend but a servant. Now while there is nothing wrong with referring to the Lord as a friend, we must readily acknowledge that our primary relationship with Him is that of a servant who was created to worship and serve Him.

2. Mary accepted God's plan as best for her life. She didn't try to argue it or try to negotiate out of it, she merely accepted it and prepared herself for the consequences of it.

Mary knew that submission was not about being "under the thumb" or about living a life without freedom and choice. She knew that submission was obedience to God, and that in choosing to obey she was honouring Him, which after all was the very reason for her existence.

God tells us in His word that we are to lovingly submit to Him, our husbands and those in authority. What is your response to that? Dear friend, choose to be the mother who replies "I am the Lord's servant, may it be to me as you have said."

*Father, thank You for Mary's example of submission, and for the Lord Jesus, who submitted to You in all things. I am ashamed of the many ways I have had a hard heart or a rebellious heart and I ask that You forgive me. Please transform my heart into that of a servant who exists only to glorify You, and to obey Your word. In Jesus' name, Amen.*

VERSES FOR FURTHER STUDY
- Ephesians 5:22-24
- Philippians 2:5-8
- 1 Peter 2:13-15

QUESTIONS FOR REFLECTION
- Why should Christians submit themselves to God?
- What in your life demonstrates submission to God? To your husband? To those in authority?
- Do you willingly submit?
- Who else in the Bible is an example to follow of a life in submission to God?
- What principles can you apply to your own life?

# 18

# The Mother Who... Trusts

*Trust in the LORD with all your heart and lean not on your own understanding;*
*in all your ways acknowledge him and he will make your paths straight.*

PROVERBS 3:5-6

Some time ago my husband and I were faced with a decision. Would we continue to explore a ministry opportunity halfway around the world from our home country, or would we return home to look for a ministry position close to our families?

For months my mind went over the positive and negative things about each scenario, wondering which situation the Lord would lead us to. Every day, both together as a couple and individually, we would pray about it, trusting that the Lord would show us the direction to take. As time went on, neither situation was "more clearly right" than the other so we made a decision to return home, trusting that the Lord would change our hearts and minds if we should be staying in the UK. Well you probably guessed it, because soon after we decided to return home to New Zealand, our hearts did an "about-turn" and we decided to accept a call to ministry in Kent, England.

In looking back over that time, I see that there were occasions that I didn't trust the Lord. I prayed "Lord we trust You to lead us to the ministry You would have for us," but in my heart there were times I felt anxious, wondering if the Lord might not clearly direct us. I see now that at times my trust in God was more about intellectual knowledge than a true practice in my life. I *knew* I could trust the Lord, but at times the attitudes of my heart proved that I did not trust Him. Since then I have had MANY opportunities to practise trusting Him – and I am sure there will be plenty more opportunities to come. If only I had got it right the first time, I wonder how much heartache I might have avoided!

But there is something that encourages me. I am not the only one who has struggled to trust the Lord. Someone else who comes to my mind is the disciple Peter. Matthew 14:22-32 tells us an account of Peter learning to trust the Lord. Do you remember it? The disciples were in a boat after Jesus told them to cross the water without Him. The winds were tossing the boat around while it was still a long distance from land. The disciples look out across the water and suddenly they are afraid because they see a figure coming towards them – walking on the water! It is Jesus and He knows they are afraid so He calls out *"Take courage! It is I. Don't be afraid."* Peter called back, *"Lord, if it's you, tell me to come to you on the water."* So Jesus replied, *"Come."* Peter stepped out of the boat and began walking on the water towards Jesus. But then he took his eyes off Jesus and became afraid of the winds and the crashing waves, and he began to sink into the water. Jesus reached out and caught Peter's hand. Then He rebuked Peter and said, *"You of little faith, why did you doubt?"*

If you are anything like me, you might have had the same question run through your mind as I did when I read that account. How on earth could Peter doubt when he not only knew Jesus to be the Son of God, but he had already seen Jesus perform many miracles? Not only that, but if he was already walking on water, why would he doubt that he couldn't keep walking towards the Lord? How much evidence did this guy need in order to trust Jesus completely?

A very similar point was made in an account Jesus told of a rich man who was in Hades, but was talking to Abraham (Luke 16:19-31). The man asked Abraham to send someone from the dead back to life to warn his family of the reality of hell. But Abraham replied *"If they do not listen to Moses and the Prophets, they will not be convinced even if someone rises from the dead"* (v. 31). They needed no more evidence than the Old Testament Scripture provided.

What does it take for us to put our trust completely in the Lord Jesus Christ?

Think back to Peter. Yes, he saw miracles performed. He saw the dead rise, the hungry fed, the sick healed, the lame walk and sins, forgiven. Peter saw that Jesus forgave people of their sins, thus ensuring them a place in heaven with Him for eternity. That's the biggest miracle of all. And if you are truly saved by grace alone through faith, then you have witnessed that very miracle too – in your very own life. What more do we need to do to trust the Lord? Nothing. We just need to obey.

Is there a situation in your life which the Lord would have you trust completely to Him? A situation which you need to trust Him *not only* with your mind, *but with your heart* as well? Dear Mother, trust in the Lord with all your heart, for He will make your paths straight.

*Father, forgive me for the many times when I have not trusted You. I know that I can trust in You, and that I am to be obedient by trusting You. Thank You for promising that You will direct*

*my paths and for the many ways You have led me. In Jesus'
name, Amen.*

## VERSES FOR FURTHER STUDY

- Psalm 20
- Psalm 56:4
- Isaiah 25:1-9
- Proverbs 28:26

## QUESTIONS FOR REFLECTION

- When do you find it difficult to trust the Lord? Why?
- What is your response to a difficult or uncertain situation?
- What daily practice can you develop to ensure that you trust the Lord with all your heart?

# 19

# The Mother Who... Serves

*...then choose for yourselves this day whom you will serve...*
JOSHUA 24:15

Imagine if this Sunday at church your pastor gathered you all together and, after reminding you of all that God has done in your lives, said to you "Choose today whom you will serve." Would that seem strange? After all, if you didn't want to serve the Lord then surely you wouldn't bother going to church, right?

He should not even have to ask.

Return now to Joshua. He did in fact do exactly that. He gathers all of the tribes of Israel together, and after reminding them all of what God had done for them, he asks them to choose whom they will serve. Why did Joshua even have to ask? Look at the verses which follow in Joshua 24:21, 23, The people say, *"We will serve the LORD."* Joshua replies to them, *"throw away the foreign gods that are among you and yield your hearts to the LORD, the God of Israel."*

We read in the Bible that God's people were a fickle people. Time and time again they turned their backs on God and served foreign and man-made gods. Think back to the time of Moses in Exodus 32. Moses was up on Mount Sinai to receive from God the Ten Commandments. While he was away doing that, the Israelites went to Moses' brother, Aaron, and said *"Come, make us gods who will go before us"*. So Aaron took all their gold and melted it together and fashioned a golden calf. The Israelites worshipped it saying *"These are your gods, O Israel, who brought you up out of Egypt"* (Exod. 32:4-6). What an incredible statement! How that must have grieved God. (As an aside, is it not ironic that the first two commandments which God gave Moses were direct commandments against serving anyone or anything other than God?)

The Israelites saw over and over the hand of God at work to deliver them from slavery and oppression. The provision of Moses to lead them. The dreadful plagues afflicted on Egypt because of Pharaoh's refusal to let them go. The parting of the Red Sea making a way of escape from Pharaoh's army. Provision of food and water in the desert for millions of people! And still they turned their backs on God, instead giving praise and worship to a calf made from their gold.

At this point it is very easy for us to make a harsh judgment about how foolish the Israelites were. But there is something that holds me back from making such a prideful response, because the truth is that we are just like the Israelites. Our hearts are just as fickle and can so easily fall into idolatry. Only we might be a little more subtle than creating a golden calf for everyone to see.

While we may not have a golden calf to bow down to, maybe there are other things or dreams of other things which cause our hearts to bow. Maybe something like a beautiful home, or a desire for a beautiful home; our husband; our children; our bodies – or desire for the perfect body; shopping; a fat bank account. Any of these things and many more, could have us so focused on them that we become followers of them instead of followers of God.

Jesus knew that we could be weak in this way and so that's why He warns us about it: *"No-one can serve two masters. Either he will hate the one and love the other, or he will be devoted to the one and despise the other. You cannot serve both God and Money"* (Matt. 6:24).

Idolatry is not a sin which is used only to describe people who outwardly worship other gods or things. It is a sin which we also can so easily fall into and at times we may not even realise it. Hold your life up to the Light of the World. Is there anything or anyone which you have allowed to take pre-eminence over Him?

Dear mother, don't be like the Israelites who allowed a man-made, self-imposed idol to rule their hearts. Choose this day that it is Jesus whom you will serve.

*Father, how we thank You for the reminder that our hearts are so shallow and fickle. Thank You for showing me how other things can so easily take Your place in my life and for warning me against it. Please forgive me for the times that I have not kept You on the throne of my heart. Please help me to guard against anything that could usurp You from your rightful place in my life, no matter how worthy or good the things are. Father, this day I choose to serve You. In Jesus' name, Amen.*

## VERSES FOR FURTHER STUDY

- Matthew 6:19-24
- Matthew 4:8-11
- Colossians 3:5

## QUESTIONS FOR REFLECTION

- Do you know of any "golden calves" in your life? If yes, what/who are they?

- How can you make sure to protect your heart from the sin of idolatry?
- What do you think are the common "golden calves" for mothers, and how can they be avoided?

# 20

# The Mother Who... Counsels

*The wise in heart are called discerning, and pleasant words promote instruction.*

Proverbs 16:21

There is just something so luxurious about going to my favourite cafe with a girlfriend and curling up in one of the overstuffed armchairs with a latte and a piece of toffee pecan slice. Why? Because I love a good catch-up and chat! I love sharing my thoughts and dreams, and sometimes my disappointments and sorrows. And I love to hear about what is happening in my friend's life. It can be such a refreshing time – but on the flip side it can also be a destructive time.

The above verse in Proverbs is just one of many which remind us to be cautious with our words. But why would we need to be cautious when we are chatting with a friend? We learn from James 3 that the tongue can cause terrible destruction; *"The tongue also is a fire, a world of evil among the parts of the body. It corrupts the whole person, sets the whole course of his life on fire, and is itself set on fire by hell"* (James 3:6). Read ahead to verses 9 and 10 and we see that *"With the tongue we praise our Lord and Father, and with it we curse men, who have been made in God's likeness. Out of the same mouth come praise and cursing. My brothers, this should not be."*

The book of James warns us of the POWER of our speech and the ruin it can cause. Proverbs reminds us that the more we talk, the more likely we are to sin with our words. *"When words are many, sin is not absent, but he who holds his tongue is wise"* (Prov. 10:19).

The Bible tells us that a godly woman doesn't gossip (Prov. 16:28), she doesn't quarrel (2 Tim. 2:23-24), and she isn't slanderous (Titus 2:3). But it can be so easy to fall into these verbal sins when we are chatting with friends. Particularly so if we are sharing the sorrows, troubles, trials, hurts and disappointments of our hearts. So then, how must we respond to a friend who unburdens her heart with us over a latte? After all, we want to be a help and not a hindrance in the work the Lord is doing in her life, right?

Proverbs 27:9 tells us that *"Perfume and incense bring joy to the heart, and the pleasantness of one's friend springs from his earnest counsel."* It is a good friend who gives wise and earnest counsel and feedback. Don't be intimidated by the word "wise". Wisdom is simply biblical truth applied. We must bring the Bible to bear on all the situations we face. We must develop a biblical world-view and use that to filter everything through.

So here are a few things to keep in mind during our girlie chat sessions.

1. We are to be honest. Speak the truth in love (Eph. 4:15). Speak gently, lovingly and kindly. Proverbs 27:6 says *"Wounds from a friend can be trusted, but an enemy multiplies kisses."*

2. We are to give hope. The Bible has the answers for all of our situations and problems (2 Tim. 3:16-17). Many

people believe that our spiritual needs can be met by the Bible but our emotional needs can only be met by the latest psychological theory and counsel. Not so! Paul tells Timothy that Scripture is sufficient!

3. We are to point our friend to Scripture. What better encouragement than to point a friend to a passage in Scripture which will encourage a burdened heart, calm anxious thoughts and give wisdom on living life as a godly woman.

4. We are to edify. *"Do not let any unwholesome talk come out of your mouths, but only what is helpful for building others up according to their needs, that it may benefit those who listen"* (Eph. 4:29).

Perhaps, like me, you feel intimidated or not equipped because of your lack of Bible knowledge or Scripture memory verses. We must remember that no-one expects us to have all the answers in our heads. But we do have the answers at our fingertips. It's an honest friend who can say "I don't know what to say about that, but let's look in the Bible and see what God has to say about it."

And finally, the very best way to use our words in counsel for our friends is in prayer, seeking counsel from the Great Counsellor Himself. What a privilege we have in being able to approach the throne of Grace, knowing that we can entrust all life's burdens, joys, disappointments and sorrows with Him.

*Father, please forgive me for the times that I have not honoured You with my speech and counsel. I pray that regardless of any counsel I have given which might be unwise and foolish, that I would not have hindered Your purposes in anyone's life. Please give me wisdom and caution in my use of words and help me to encourage and edify others for Your glory. In Jesus' name, Amen.*

VERSES FOR FURTHER STUDY
- James 1:2-6
- 2 Timothy 3:16-17
- 1 Kings 22:5
- Proverbs 15:22
- Isaiah 9:6

QUESTIONS FOR REFLECTION
- Are you someone people turn to when they need to talk? Why or why not?
- How would you describe advice you give to friends who are experiencing difficulties in their lives?
- What Bible verses or passages could you use to encourage a friend who is struggling in the area of submission to her husband/assurance of her salvation/ loss of a family member?
- Why is our Lord described as "Wonderful Counsellor" in Isaiah 9:6

# 21

# The Mother Who... Forgives

*Bear with each other and forgive whatever grievances you may have against one another. Forgive as the Lord forgave you.*

COLOSSIANS 3:13

I stood at my husband's desk fuming as he apologized to me. I knew this was the time for me to say "I forgive you" but my lips remained tightly pressed together. I was torn – not only was I aware I was also to blame for this situation, but I knew that I had often wronged him and had met with forgiveness. Still, the temptation remained to punish him just a little so he wouldn't make the same mistake twice. Perhaps you have been faced with the same temptation, to just wait a little while until the lesson is learned before you extend the sceptre of forgiveness.

However, the Bible tells us that we are to forgive straight away, not after a lesson has been learned and the offender has been punished. In fact the above verses don't even speak of punishment – they simply say "forgive". It's a command to us – not an option if and when we feel like it. What happens if we don't obey a command of the Lord? We are sinning. The Apostle helps us out of the struggle with this by reminding us that not only are we to "forgive" but we are to forgive as the

Lord forgives us. Well I guess that puts it into perspective. The Lord Jesus not only forgave us our sin, but He gave His life to take the punishment that we deserve. But even though we know all this, we still struggle to forgive others when they wrong us.

Let's look at another example of some who struggled to forgive. In Luke 6:6-11 we read an account of Jesus healing a man's crippled hand on the Sabbath. The Pharisees were furious about it and began discussing what they could do to Him. Why were they doing that? Because they could not forgive Jesus. Doesn't that seem like a ridiculous statement? Why on earth would Jesus need to be forgiven? After all, He is God – sinless, faultless, Saviour, Redeemer. Therein lies the problem. The Pharisees were furious and unforgiving towards Jesus because He had challenged their authority, revealing their legalistic religiosity and self-idolatry. Jesus' very presence lifted the veil of their hardened and sinful hearts for everyone to see. Jesus said to the Pharisees, *"Now then, you Pharisees clean the outside of the cup and dish, but inside you are full of greed and wickedness. You foolish people! Did not the one who made the outside make the inside also?"* (Luke 11:39-40). He also warned His disciples about the Pharisees, saying *"Be on your guard against the yeast of the Pharisees, which is hypocrisy. There is nothing concealed that will not be disclosed, or hidden that will not be made known"* (Luke 12:1-2).

Jesus exposes hardened and unforgiving hearts. The Pharisees could have repented and received eternal life, but instead they had unforgiving hearts. Sadly, the eternal destination for those with hardened hearts towards the Lord is not heaven but hell. *"Woe to you experts in the law, because you have taken away the key to knowledge. You yourselves have not entered, and you have hindered those who were entering"* (Luke 11:52).

Unforgiveness is a serious sin! Jesus again highlights this in the parable of the unmerciful servant (Matt. 18:21-35). This servant owed his master a great deal of money and the master, in compassion, freed him from the debt. The servant then comes upon someone who owes him a small amount of money. He demands the money from him, but he is unable to pay, so the servant has him dragged off to prison. When the master found out about this he ordered the same treatment to be given to the servant, because the servant showed an unforgiving heart. Jesus concludes the parable by saying *"This is how my heavenly Father will treat each of you unless you forgive your brother from your heart"* (v. 35). That is an absolutely frightening thought. And yet ... we still struggle to forgive!

What else does the Bible say about our struggle to forgive? James 4:12 tells us, *"There is only one Lawgiver and Judge, the one who is able to save and destroy. But you – who are you to judge your neighbour?"*

Jesus is the only Judge, which means that He will also seek justice and retribution. It's not our job! All we need to do is obey. Just forgive ... and forget.

*Father, thank You for Your Son Jesus, who came to this world that I might be forgiven and set free from sin. Lord sometimes it is so hard to forgive, even though I know that You forgive me so freely. Please help me not be a Pharisee and be proud and hard of heart, but to forgive freely as You forgive me. In Jesus' name, Amen.*

## VERSES FOR FURTHER STUDY

- Psalm 130:3-4
- Nehemiah 9:16-31

QUESTIONS FOR REFLECTION

- What has Jesus forgiven you for recently?
- When people ask you for forgiveness, or even if they don't ask, do you give it freely?
- What causes you to struggle with forgiveness?
- What does the Bible say about such things?

# 22

# The Mother Who... Is Content

*...I have learned to be content whatever the circumstances.*

PHILIPPIANS 4:11B

Let me ask you something. What is the one thing that would complete your happiness?

I imagine some answers might be quite "spiritual". For example, "That I would no longer struggle with the sin of gossip," or "That my husband/children would be saved." And then I am sure there would be some "not-so-spiritual" answers. "To lose weight," "To have enough money to do whatever we wanted," "That my husband would give me the respect I deserve." And then perhaps some might say, as the Apostle Paul said "I have learned to be content whatever the circumstances."

I am not saying that any of the so-called spiritual or "not-so-spiritual" answers are wrong. However, our sinful hearts are lying to us if they tell us that we need these things to be truly content. This is a concept that I continually need to remind myself of. As a young woman trying to raise a family on the other side of the world from "home," I sometimes find myself thinking that I would be truly happy if we could just be near our family and friends. But it's not true! Our greedy hearts will always hunger for more.

A very wealthy man was asked "How much money is enough?" He replied "Just a little more." That reminds me of the rich young man in Mark 10:17-31. He asked Jesus, *"What must I do to inherit eternal life?"* Jesus told him, *"Go sell everything you have and give to the poor, and you will have treasure in heaven. Then come, follow me."* It then goes on to say that the young man *"went away sad, because he had great wealth."* Jesus was not saying that to become a Christian the young man had to become poor. He was making the point that the young man's wealth was an idol of his heart – and what is the first commandment that God gave the Israelites? *"You shall have no other gods before me"* (Deut. 5:7). The young man had made an idol of wealth and did not believe he could be content without it.

That is what we must ask ourselves when we are struggling with discontentment. "What or who is my heart longing after – besides a closer walk with God?"

Think back to the Apostle Paul. What are these circumstances that he had learned to be content in? *"I know what it is to be in need, and I know what it is to have plenty. I have learned the secret of being content in any and every situation, whether well fed or hungry, whether living in plenty or in want"* (Phil. 4:12). Paul was shipwrecked, imprisoned, chained and flogged, beaten and stoned. He also wrote the following words: *"For to me, to live is Christ and to die is gain"* (Phil. 1:21). Paul lived for nothing more than to serve the Lord.

I wonder if this is convicting you as it is me right now? Paul suffered shocking persecution just because he was a Christian who was not ashamed to serve the Lord. He had no home to call his own, no regular income, no companionship through many difficult days, and even at times not enough food to eat or clothing to wear. And yet he learned to be content in all these situations. What is his secret to contentment? *"I can do everything through him who gives me strength"* (Phil. 4:13). That's the secret. Not relying on our own willpower or strength but being fully reliant on God in all that we do.

This means we are to rid ourselves of any idols of the heart. Think back to the rich young man who wouldn't give up his love of wealth and money. Is there anything in your life which you need to give up in order that God has first priority in your heart? Don't forget, you can do all things through Him who gives you strength. What a joy to be a mother who is truly content!

> *Father, please forgive my discontented heart which hungers for more and more. I know that nothing aside from You can truly satisfy my heart's desires. Thank You for Paul's example to us of contentment regardless of the situations he faced. Please help me to learn contentment and to be able to find my strength in You. In Jesus' name, Amen.*

VERSES FOR FURTHER STUDY
- Philippians 3: 8-9
- Matthew 8:18-22
- Matthew 19:27-29
- 1 Timothy 6:6-11

QUESTIONS FOR REFLECTION
- Can you identify any idols of the heart in your own life which cause you discontentment?
- What part do the media play in contributing to discontentment? How can you best deal with influence from the media?
- It has been said that window-shopping breeds discontentment. What else in your life causes discontentment? How can you avoid it or deal with it?

# 23

# The Mother Who... Is Modest

*I also want women to dress modestly, with decency and propriety,
not with braided hair or gold or pearls or expensive clothes,
but with good deeds, appropriate for women who profess to worship God.*

1 Timothy 2:9-10

There's a saying that goes "if you've got it, flaunt it!" Sadly, it seems the world has taken this to heart because everywhere we look we see that the god of fashion has a large band of followers who are indeed "flaunting it."

Women and girls in clothing that is too short, too high, too low, too tight, low-cut, high-cut and shamelessly revealing are parading themselves not only on the television and billboards, but on the streets, in the malls, in restaurants and even in churches when they gather to worship God. In fact I heard someone say recently that if women 100 years ago wore what some women wear today to church, they would have been arrested! The only thing which should expose us in church is the Word of God which reveals our hearts.

What else does the Bible say of women who are dressed inappropriately? Proverbs 7 tells us of a woman who was dressed to seek attention from a man so she could then entice him and seduce him: *"Then out came a woman to meet him, dressed like a prostitute and with crafty intent"* (Prov. 7:10).

The Bible gives warnings to men about such women: *"Do not lust in your heart after her beauty or let her captivate you with her eyes"* (Prov. 6:25).

These two verses reveal a woman intent on capturing a man's attention through the way she presents her body. In fact the first verse likens her to a prostitute because of the clothes she wears.

Revealing clothes and inappropriate dress reveal and draw attention not only to her body but also to her heart. It reveals an attention-seeking heart instead of a God-focused heart; a prideful heart, not a humble heart; a sinful heart, not a pure heart.

There is no surprise that the world's definition of beauty is so different from what God thinks is beautiful. Paul warns us of this in a letter to the church at Colosse: *"See to it that no-one takes you captive through hollow and deceptive philosophy, which depends on human tradition and the basic principles of this world rather than on Christ"* (Col. 2:8).

The "less is more" fashion and beauty philosophy is not the only "hollow and deceptive" philosophy we come up against as Christians.

Consider the difference of that philosophy to just four things I have listed which God considers beautiful.

1. Good deeds (1 Tim. 2:10).
2. A gentle and quiet spirit (1 Pet. 3:3-4).
3. Fear of the Lord (Prov. 31:30).
4. Obedience (Rom. 12:1-2).

Sadly, it would seem that some Christian women think that honouring the Lord with their body is optional. Question them on it and you might be accused of being old-fashioned, prudish or out of touch. However, this is a topic that the Bible addresses specifically and clearly. We know that beauty is not about outward adornment, the latest fashion or the cutest haircut. And neither is it wrong to look nice and enjoy nice clothes, accessories and a nice haircut. The Proverbs 31 woman was known for her beautiful quality clothing (Prov. 31:22). What Paul is telling us in the verses in 1 Timothy is that true beauty is a heart issue. A heart which longs to give glory to God, to be renewed and transformed by the Word, to worship God and seek after purity, is the standard of beauty we should be seeking after. It is of great worth in God's eyes. There's nothing more beautiful than that!

*Father, thank You for the clear and specific teaching in Your Word not only about how we are to dress, but also the standard of beauty we are to attain to. Please help me to reflect a life which worships You by the way that I dress and present myself. I pray that when people look at me they would see nothing more than a woman who worships God. In Jesus' name, Amen.*

VERSES FOR FURTHER STUDY

- 1 Peter 3:3-5
- Proverbs 31:30
- Proverbs 11:22
- Matthew 26:10

QUESTIONS FOR REFLECTION

- What is the world's definition or philosophy of beautiful?
- Has that in any way impacted your own dress and fashion sense?
- How does your standard of dress measure up to what the Lord expects from a godly woman?

- Is there anything that you need to address in your life so that you are considered beautiful in God's eyes and not the eyes of the world?

## 24

# The Mother Who... Listens

*She had a sister called Mary, who sat at the Lord's feet listening to what he said.*

Luke 10:39

Come back about 2,000 years with me. Jesus and His disciples were journeying when they came to a village which was home to the sisters Mary and Martha. I'm sure you know the rest of the story. Martha invited the Lord and His disciples to her home for hospitality. She began making preparations for her large group of guests but her sister Mary just sat at the feet of the Lord, listening to His teaching. This is where it gets interesting. Logic would say that Martha would be feeling perhaps a little stressed. She had at least thirteen guests and it seems like she had no other help with the preparations. But the Bible doesn't speak of Martha being stressed, or overburdened or even busy. It speaks of her being "distracted." Luke 10:40 says *"Martha was distracted by all the preparations that had to be made."* Distracted from what? Read verse 39 again. *"She had a sister called Mary, who sat at the Lord's feet listening to what He said."* Martha was distracted from listening to Jesus.

I wonder if Martha was just so distracted by all the preparations she was making for her guests that she didn't even know that Jesus had something to say to her. Can you imagine it? Jesus turns up at your home with His disciples, so of course you invite them in. They've walked great distances and have been so busy in ministry, so you decide they need a good meal and a good rest. Yep – it's easy to see how the preparations became distracting from everything else that was happening in the house! Except we have missed a very important detail. The main guest who had arrived wasn't just an old friend from out of town. It was the Son of God. Maybe you're thinking "Yeah but Martha didn't really understand that back then." Maybe so – but how come thousands of others understood it?

Think back to chapter nine in the gospel of Luke. Crowds of people followed Jesus so they could listen to His teaching. In fact Luke 9:10-17 tells us how Jesus fed five thousand people. All of these folk had followed Jesus to hear His teaching and then it came time to eat. Interestingly, not one of these five thousand had organised hospitality for their speaker, or even for themselves. They had the very Bread of Life in their midst! So how come these five thousand knew that Jesus was someone to listen to but Martha didn't?

Here are a few thoughts.

## 1. Martha was worried.

Isn't it true that when we are worried or anxious or upset about something, it takes over our thoughts and emotions? That's why the Bible says *"Do not be anxious about anything, but in everything, by prayer and petition, with thanksgiving, present your requests to God"* (Phil. 4:6).

That's not just a suggestion to us. It's a command. Worrying is sinful!

## 2. Martha had a self-important attitude.

*"Lord, don't you care that my sister has left me to do the work by myself? Tell her to help me!"* (Luke 10:40).

The truth is that Martha actually didn't need to be so busy with the preparations. As we have already recalled, the Lord had recently fed over five thousand people with just five loaves of bread and two fish. If she had thought it through, she would have known that Jesus could have performed a miracle and provided all that they needed and more. Martha was too busy focusing on herself and her self-appointed role of hostess instead of focusing on the Son of God.

## 3. Martha chose the wrong option.

Martha should not have been distracted, and nor should she have tried to distract her sister by trying to get her working too. Did you know that Mary is the same Mary who in John 12 poured a very expensive bottle of perfume over Jesus' feet? Oh how Mary loved Jesus! But what was Martha doing whilst Mary showed her love to the Lord? She was ... serving the meal. There is nothing wrong with serving a meal – it can certainly be a way of showing love. But again, how did Martha get caught up in a mundane task while the Son of God was in her home? We see here in Luke 10 the same thing. Mary shows her love for the Lord by listening to Him – and what does Martha do? She gets cross and worried and distracted in trying to serve Him. Mary chose the better way!

There is much for us to learn from Mary and Martha. Dear mother, I know how busy your day is (and probably your evening, late night, early morning ...) but we need to choose to push aside all that is distracting us from spending time with the Lord. The mother who listens to Him is the mother who has chosen what is better.

*Father, there are often times when, because of the choices I have made, I am too busy to listen to You. Please forgive me and help me to be like Mary, to know what is best. Help me not to allow my service to You to become a sacrifice of my time with You. Lord I want to choose the better way. In Jesus' name, Amen.*

## VERSES FOR FURTHER STUDY
- Proverbs 1:5
- John 10:27
- James 1:22-25

## QUESTIONS FOR REFLECTION
- Which sister can you relate more to and why?
- How can you best organize your day so that you can set regular time aside for the Lord?
- What most commonly distracts you from your time with the Lord? What can you do about it?

# 25

# The Mother Who... Is Still

> Be still, and know that I am God.
> Psalm 46:10

I know, I know! You probably read the title of today's devotional and laughed. You're thinking "That sentence is an oxymoron, unless the word 'never' is added." I know that certainly *this* mother *is never* still!

However, God says *"Be still, and know that I am God."*

I don't know that I had ever really put a whole lot of thought into that verse. Yes I've sung the well-known song hundreds of times and every time I do I affirm with my heart that He is God. But have I taken time to really *know* it? I'm not sure that I have, and perhaps you may not have either. So I spent some time thinking through some other verses in my Bible which describe God so that we might know Him better. Here is just some of what I found.

## 1. God is the One True God.

In the days of Moses leading the Israelites out of Egypt, Moses told them that many of the mighty and miraculous things that they saw God do were so that they might know *"that the Lord is God; besides Him there is no other"* (Deut. 4:35). Why did he tell them that? We find out a few verses later in verse 39: *"Acknowledge and take to heart this day that the LORD is God in heaven above and on the earth below. There is no other. Keep His decrees and commands..."* There is a connection. Once we have acknowledged that God is the One True God and taken to heart what that means, we then have a responsibility to live our lives in obedience to Him.

The God we know expects obedience from His children.

## 2. God is our refuge and strength (Ps. 46:1).

Just as David was comforted by these attributes so too should we be. Though David's life was very different to ours, he still experienced many situations which we can relate to. He suffered grief, loneliness, separation from loved ones, a job which seemed so overwhelming and out of his league (have you ever faced a murderous giant with only a few stones and a slingshot to protect you?). I recently heard someone say that the Christian life is such that you are either in a trial, have just come through a trial or are about to enter a trial! But don't be afraid. The God we know is our refuge and strength.

## 3. God is Sovereign.

When Daniel was interpreting King Nebuchadnezzar's dream he told the King that he must acknowledge that God is sovereign over kingdoms and gives them to anyone he wishes (Dan. 4:25).

Nothing can happen in our lives, our country, our world, our government, which God has not allowed to happen. And because we know that to be true, we can affirm *"we know that in all things God works for the good of those who love him, who have been called according to His purpose"* (Rom. 8:28). God uses all circumstances in the believer's life to grow them and change them more and more into His likeness. That's liberating isn't it? We can relax because the God we know is in control.

## 4. God sent His Son to die for our sins (John 3:16).

Knowing this to be true has all sorts of implications for our lives. In what way? Well, it demands a response. For example, what do you do when someone gives you a gift? I would imagine that you respond by saying thank you. So then, what are we to do when the one and only Son of God dies a hideous death so that we might be forgiven our sins and be able to freely enter into a right relationship with God? We are to live a life of thanks and praise to God. Our hearts should be overflowing with worship, humility, gratitude. We should be keen evangelists, humble servants transformed in our attitudes, speech and behaviour. That shouldn't be too hard because the God we know sacrificed His only Son in order that we might live.

After thinking through just four things which help me to know God, I wonder if I truly do know Him. Not in the sense that I don't think that I am saved, I know that I am for sure. But in the sense that as I look at my life I wonder why I so often fail to live like I truly know that He is God. I so often let Him down. But then, do you know something else so great about our God? The God that we know is a forgiving God.

What a privilege it is to be a mother who can be still and know that He is God.

*Father, how humbled I am to be Your child. You are the One True God and besides You there is no other. Thank You for being my refuge and strength. Thank You that You are sovereign over all circumstances that surround our lives. Thank You for giving Your Son that I might live. Please help me to live for You. In Jesus' name, Amen.*

Verses for Further Study

- Exodus 3:1-15
- 1 Kings 18:16-39
- Ezekiel 36:23

Questions for Reflection

- What other attributes of God can you list?
- What is your response to each attribute?
- Why do we need to be reminded to *"Be still, and know that I am God"*?
- What do you need to do in your life to make sure you continue living in a way that shows you know God?

## 26

# The Mother Who... Prays

*The LORD is far from the wicked but he hears the prayer of the righteous.*
PROVERBS 15:29

Have you ever considered the reality of Proverbs 15:29? The Lord, the Creator of the universe, the Almighty and Sovereign God actually listens to our prayers. Wow! Does that change anything for you with regard to your prayer life? It certainly does for me. In fact, it makes me feel more urgency in my need to *"pray continually"* (1 Thess. 5:17). Not pray literally twenty four hours a day, seven days a week. That's impossible. But certainly it does mean that we are to pray persistently and regularly.

As mothers we have an awesome responsibility to pray for our children. For their safety and wellbeing, for their salvation, their spiritual maturity and growth, their respect and awe of God, their hunger for biblical truth, their education, their futures, possible future spouses and children. Actually, maybe we do need to pray continually just to cover all of that! Suddenly prayer seems overwhelming. Before we know it we have allowed our prayer time to be one of those activities that we know we should be doing but which seem too hard and time-consuming and overwhelming.

Sound familiar? Dear mother, prayer is an absolute necessity in our lives and for the lives of those we pray for. Let's look together at some truths about prayer which will reignite our passion for prayer.

## 1. God is pleased by our prayer

Proverbs 15:8 says, *"The LORD detests the sacrifice of the wicked but the prayer of the upright pleases him."* When we pray as God would have us pray, with a pure heart, honestly seeking after His will for all of our requests, it pleases God. So when we pray for our child's salvation, it pleases God. In fact, the New King James Bible uses the word "delight" instead of "pleases".

Doesn't it delight you to know that by praying with a pure heart, you delight Him?

## 2. God answers prayer

*"Until now you have not asked for anything in my name. Ask and you will receive, and your joy will be complete"*

(John 16:24)

Do you know what it is to ask in Jesus' name? It is to ask for whatever is within the will and purpose of Jesus in a person's life. So when we end our prayer by saying "In Jesus' name" we are really saying "Because it is in accordance with Jesus' will." Isn't that an encouragement! God will only answer prayer if it is in accordance with what Jesus wills for a person.

## 3. God uses prayer for our growth

*"If any of you lacks wisdom, he should ask God, who gives generously to all without finding fault, and it will be given to him. But when he asks, he must believe and not doubt, because he who doubts is like a wave of the sea, blown and tossed by the wind"*

(James 1:5-6)

These verses are just one example of how God uses prayer to grow us in qualities needed to be more like Him. Have you ever thought about the qualities prayer develops? Here are a few: Perseverance, patience, humility, hunger for the truth and knowledge of God's will, reliance on God and not on others. Wow! Let's get praying!

## 4. God uses prayer to comfort us

> *"Do not be anxious about anything, but in everything, by prayer and petition, with thanksgiving, present your requests to God. And the peace of God, which transcends all understanding, will guard your hearts and your minds in Christ Jesus."*
>
> (Phil. 4:6-7)

> *"Come to me, all you who are weary and burdened, and I will give you rest"*
>
> (Matt. 11:28).

These are just a few examples of the comfort we receive from God through prayer.

Prayer really is more than just a quick, one-sided conversation with God, isn't it? It's about relationship. A relationship which not only involves us and God, but also the ones we pray for. Prayer is a rich gift to give but the rewards we reap from praying are even richer!

> *Father God, how good it is to come into Your presence and open our hearts to You. Thank You for the privilege of prayer and the work that You accomplish through it in my life and the lives of others. I again commit my children to You now and ask for Your truth to permeate into their lives that they might receive You as their Lord and Saviour. Please forgive my lack of prayer and help me to give it the priority in my life that I need it to have. In Jesus' name, Amen.*

Verses for Further Study
- Matthew 6:5-13
- Romans 8:26-27
- James 5:13-16

Questions for Reflection
- How would you describe your prayer life?
- How can you pray more effectively with the time you have?
- What three things can you pray specifically and regularly for in your children's lives?
- How can you encourage the prayer lives of your children?

## 27

# The Mother Who... Is Busy

*She watches over the affairs of her household and does not eat the bread of idleness.*

PROVERBS 31:27

You've heard the saying "Do you want to speak to the man in charge or to the woman who knows what's happening?"

While this is meant in many ways to be derogatory, there is an element of truth to it.

While the man is the head of the home, it is generally the woman who is the centre of the home. She is the one who organizes her day around music practice, brownies, football practice, youth group, coffee morning, school trips, church activities and so on. Not to mention keeping her home clean, providing meals for her family, and hopefully somewhere in there, spending some quality time with each of her family members and her Lord. There may even be paid employment in there too. Not many paid jobs would involve such a hectic, demanding and multi-skilled schedule!

Sadly the feminist movement would have us believe that the role of a homemaker is a "no-brainer." Apparently it's a job which can only be described as unsatisfying, unimportant and unpopular. Ironically, because of the rise in numbers of women who are working outside of the home, there is now the need for "professional childminders". Women now get paid to go to work to look after other people's children in order that those women might ... go to work!

However, homemaking and motherhood is commended to us by the Lord. The Proverbs 31 woman is praised not only by her husband and her children, but also by her God. And if ever there was a busy woman, here she is! Read Proverbs 31:10-31 and look at the tasks she is involved in. Does she seem unfulfilled? Discontented? In need of some "me time" or a chance to "use her brain"? I think the only thing she is in need of is a holiday! Look at some of the words used to describe her busy day: *"She... works with **eager** hands"* (v. 13), *"She **considers** a field and buys it"* (v. 16), *"She sets about her work **vigorously**"* (v. 17), *"She is clothed with **strength** and **dignity**; she can **laugh** at days to come"* (v. 25), *"She speaks with **wisdom**"* (v. 26).

There is nothing here which suggests this full-time mother spends her days being bored, unfulfilled, or unhappy. In fact, she is just the opposite. This woman is eager, thoughtful, vigorous, strong, dignified, wise and entrepreneurial as she serves her family and her Lord. Another word which describes her is **busy!**

Think briefly of another woman who is also busy serving. Think of Martha in Luke 10:38-42. Did she display all these qualities of the Proverbs 31 woman? She might have but we aren't told. However there are three words which are used to describe Martha. They are distracted, worried and upset.

Martha highlights a trap which we can so easily fall into. While we might be incredibly busy as a mother, perhaps the list of words describing us would be more similar to Martha than the Proverbs 31 woman. Maybe words like ... tired, irritable, complaining, sighing, depressed, jealous, resentful ... any of these ring true to you at times? I know there are times when I could put my name next to more than one of those words. And I also know how the impact of this on my family's life can only be negative. Why is it that our busy and often hectic days as mothers reveal in us such dreadful sins and sinful attitudes? I wonder if it's because we have forgotten whom we truly serve. Colossians 3:17 says *"And whatever you do, whether in word or deed, do it all in the name of the Lord Jesus, giving thanks to God the Father through Him."*

We are to display attitudes and actions, and speak words that are true of one who is a child of God. If we truly are His child then our hearts are transformed and His desires become our desires. What is His desire for us as mothers? To perform this role with absolute excellence in our attitudes, actions and words, just as the Proverbs 31 woman did. Yes, we are still sinners, but as my husband says "Christians aren't sinless, but they will sin less."

This season of our lives is indeed a busy one. However as Ecclesiastes 9:10 says *"Whatever your hand finds to do, do it with all your might, for in the grave, where you are going, there is neither working nor planning nor knowledge nor wisdom."* Be encouraged that this busy season of your life is exactly where the Lord would have you serve for now. It will be over all too soon but the influence you can have on your family's life right now can have eternal significance.

*Father, this is a busy time of life and some days the busyness seems to become such a chore. Please forgive me for the times when I have struggled on without turning to You for strength and wisdom. Please forgive my selfishness and at times my attitudes of self-pity. I now commit all my daily tasks to You, asking that You would help me to achieve all that I need to, making the most of every moment. And Lord please help me to be wise and discerning in the influence this precious time will have over the lives of my family. In Jesus' name, Amen.*

## VERSES FOR FURTHER STUDY

- Proverbs 31:10-31
- Luke 10: 38-42

## QUESTIONS FOR REFLECTION

- What words would describe you throughout your busy day?
- How does your busy day affect your time and relationships with the Lord and your family?
- Which quality of the Proverbs 31 woman would you most like to copy in your life? How will you do it?

# 28

# The Mother Who... Hopes

*But those who hope in the LORD will renew their strength*
Isaiah 40:31

"I hope it doesn't rain tomorrow," "I hope they have those jeans in my size," "I hope the Doctor doesn't have bad news for me," "I hope we can buy a bigger house...," "I hope...," "I hope...," "I hope..."

I think women hope a lot. We look forward into the future and hope for certain things to happen. We look back into the past and hope that certain things won't happen as a result of past decisions. But in this hope we are never certain. And in this hope we fret and worry and toss and turn at night as our strength is sapped by the uncertainty of "I hope."

Is this familiar to you? I have to say that I have been all too guilty of spending too much time looking into the future placing my hopes on things that I want to happen. But like the house that stood on the "sandy lands," placing my hopes on my dreams sent me falling with a crash. Dreams are not a firm foundation on which to place our hopes.

We have been serving the Lord away from our home country for over four years now. While I thank the Lord for the opportunity to serve in England, I also look forward to times in New Zealand with our families and friends. But sometimes it's more than just looking forward to seeing them. Sometimes it is a longing to spend time with them, to be able to watch our children play together, thinking how fun it would be having family to our home for a meal. It was really to the point that my hopes for the future were pinned on happy times with family. Then the unthinkable happened. Last year, one of my dear brothers died as a result of a car accident, leaving behind his family. Dreams and hopes of happy times suddenly shattered as grief seeped through my being. Yes there are still happy times to be had with family, but those occasions will always be marked by an underlying grief and memory of someone missing.

The future is absolutely uncertain. We do not know what the future holds even five minutes from now. We cannot place our hope on uncertainties because the foundation of such things will be sure to cause a great fall. Of course we can anticipate, with joy, times ahead with our loved ones. But we need to place our hope on what we know is sure. And what joy we have in knowing that **true** hope is certain. We do not need to hope for a bright future as Christian women because **we have** that hope. We do not have to hope that we will spend eternity with Christ because if we are saved **we have** that hope.

Notice the difference in the two kinds of hopes. One is unsure and saps our strength; the other is certain and renews our strength. Will our children join us in the family of God? Will we be struck by illness, financial difficulty or disaster? We cannot know. But what we do know is that we have the wonderful promise of salvation. We can know that our sins are forgiven and that one day we will be eternally with Him. And we can know that our Heavenly Father will hear all of what our hearts cry out to Him about all of these unknowns. He loves and cares for us and for our families more than we ever could. Doesn't your soul feel the relief of the certainty of that Hope? Does it not lift your spirit as you put your hope in the Lord – not in your circumstances, in your family or in yourself? Say that verse with your name

"_____" who hopes in the Lord will renew her strength. It's true.

> *Father thank You for the certainty that You give when we place our hope solely in You. Please forgive me for hoping in other things or other people and help me to place my hope in You always. Please renew my strength that I may daily serve You well. In Jesus' name, Amen.*

VERSES FOR FURTHER STUDY
- Psalm 42:5
- Psalm 62:5
- Proverbs 13:12
- 1 Timothy 6:17

QUESTIONS FOR REFLECTION
- In what or whom do you place your hope?
- What causes us to place our hope in things other than in God?
- How does your hope in the Lord give you strength in your day-to-day life?

## 29

# The Mother Who... Is Wise

*Wisdom is supreme; therefore get wisdom.*
*Though it cost all you have, get understanding.*
PROVERBS 4:7

As a child, my favourite books were the L M Montgomery *Anne of Green Gables* series. The red-headed orphan, Anne Shirley, was a remarkably intelligent girl who managed to achieve first equal with her sworn enemy, Gilbert Blythe, during their school years and later their college years. But however intelligent Anne was, she could not hide the fact that she was quite a silly girl whose world revolved around misplaced ideas on love and romance.

When her "bosom buddy", Diana, became engaged to local boy Fred, Anne was bitterly disappointed. She could not believe that Diana had given up her dream (really Anne's dream) of marrying someone who was ruggedly handsome, melancholy, who could be wicked if he wanted to be but of course would choose not to be, for plain, sensible, homely looking Fred! Although intelligent, Anne certainly lacked wisdom!

King Solomon, however, is reported to be the wisest king in history. How did he get to be so wise? Before we answer that, let's take a step back and find out a little more about the man Solomon. Solomon was the son of King David. What footsteps to follow! David was known as "the man after God's own heart," he was a mighty and successful king, a loving shepherd. So Solomon knew that filling the role his father had passed on to him was an awesome responsibility. One night the Lord appeared to Solomon in a dream and said to him *"Ask for whatever you want me to give you"* (1 Kings 3:5). Imagine that! The very world and all its power, wealth and resources lay at Solomon's feet! All he had to do was ask for it.

What would you do if God appeared to you in a dream and asked you that very same question? It would be nice to think that we would all respond in a selfless way, but chances are that some of us might think in terms of financial security, health, happiness and success. What did Solomon ask for?

> *"Now, O LORD my God, you have made your servant king in place of my father David. But I am only a little child and do not know how to carry out my duties. So give your servant a discerning heart to govern your people and to distinguish between right and wrong"*
>
> (1 Kings 3:7, 9).

Wow! Solomon asked for wisdom. And as we can read in verses 16-28, God gave it to him. You remember the time when Solomon showed great wisdom in settling a dispute between two women? The Bible says *"When all Israel heard the verdict the king had given, they held the king in awe, because they saw that he had wisdom from God to administer justice"* (1 Kings 3:28).

While there may not be many similarities between being a king and being a mother, there are two very important things which are exactly the same.

1.  God has called us to the role of motherhood just as he called Solomon to the role of king.
2.  A king and a mother are both servants of God and should carry out their roles with excellence and wisdom.

To be the mother who seeks after God involves immense wisdom. We are raising our children in a world where our Christian morals and biblical standards are not only frowned upon by the world but in some places we can even face legal charges under "freedom of speech" laws, smacking legislation and so on. Wisdom is absolutely essential if we are to raise godly children in an ungodly world.

Maybe you are thinking "Yeah but God gave Solomon wisdom". My friend, God has given you wisdom too. His Word, the Holy Bible is *"...God-breathed and is useful for teaching, rebuking, correcting and training in righteousness, so that the man of God may be thoroughly equipped for every good work"* (2 Tim. 3:16-17).

Delve deeply into His Word, study it and allow God to give you His wisdom for raising a family that glorifies Him. Don't settle for worldly wisdom in this important matter of child rearing. Seek only after God's wisdom, the only true wisdom and all that we need to be the mother who is wise.

*Father, thank You for the lessons which we can learn from Your Word, the Bible. It is such a joy and a privilege to be a mother, but Father it is a task which requires much wisdom and understanding. Please help me to understand and apply Your Word faithfully and wisely. Please help me to be a wise mother as I deal with the day-to-day issues, many of which can have long-term consequences. Please give my children a heart which seeks after Your wisdom and understanding.*
*In Jesus' name, Amen.*

VERSES FOR FURTHER STUDY
- James 1:5
- James 3:13-18
- Proverbs 10:13
- Proverbs 31:26

QUESTIONS FOR REFLECTION
- Read again 1 Kings 3:28. Can people see God's wisdom at work in your life as you carry out your role as a mother?
- What are the qualities that a wise mother displays?
- In what areas of your life do you need the Lord to give you wisdom?
- Pray about these things now.

# 30

# The Mother Who... Fears The Lord

> Charm is deceptive, and beauty is fleeting,
> but a woman who fears the LORD is to be praised.
>
> PROVERBS 31:30

Did you ever have a school teacher that you both adored and yet feared? The very thought of approaching that teacher gave you a feeling in the pit of your stomach and yet you really longed for some attention or some praise from them. I remember that feeling very well. In fact, I think I can remember a few teachers like that. I also remember other kids in my class trying to get attention. They would try to charm by cute comments and playing the clown. But that was never what these teachers were looking for. All they wanted was the work done and handed in on time, and if you didn't do it – then look out!

In a very simplistic way of thinking, that is what comes to mind when I think of what it means to fear the Lord. It's that mixture of fear and awe. For many people, fearing the Lord means being afraid of the punishment they think will follow if they do something "bad." They have in their heads an image of a grumpy old man, looking for any opportunity to punish them and ruin their fun. But instead we need to think on this: Jesus Christ was sent into the world by His Father, God, to live as a man and to die on a cross, and in doing so He took the punishment for all our sins. Why? He did it so that we might have eternal life with Him. He chose to do it even though we really deserved to be treated as He treated the people of Sodom and Gomorrah. Or the people of Noah's time, all killed in a great flood that covered the world because they did not have the fear of the Lord in their lives. But – even though we deserved that treatment He chose instead to die for us so that we might be forgiven.

What response is running through your mind right now? Perhaps it's admiration, respect, awe, disbelief and maybe even fear. Fear, not because God is going to treat you as you deserve, but fear because you know that He could – but He doesn't. Fear, because you want to give Him your very best to try and somehow repay Him for all that He has done for you – but all the while knowing that your best will never be enough. And fear because you know that probably every day, maybe even more than once, you will let Him down and hurt Him – even though you don't want to. That is the JOY of fearing God. It is the point where the knowledge of what God has done for you moves down from your head and into your heart and from it comes a deep longing, a response and a need to serve Him with deep respect, deep love and a deep desire to please Him.

But why is all that so praiseworthy? Why not praise all that we do for Him? All the committees we serve on, all the sacrifices we have made, the Sunday School classes we might teach or the meals we have made and served to others. Or even the amount of people we pray for or the time we spend reading our Bible? At least most of this stuff can be measured and seen. Isn't that how today's society works? Measure everything and make everything tangible?

Why is the woman who fears the Lord to be praised? Because it's about her heart attitude. Think back to 1 Samuel 16 when Samuel anointed David to be the next king of Israel. Samuel looked over David's brothers for the Lord's anointed one. What was He looking for? Maybe a strong, solidly built man with handsome features, a winning smile and a firm handshake. From my very limited knowledge of politics and government, it would seem that these qualities sure win a lot of votes! But the Lord said to Samuel *"Do not consider his appearance or his height... The LORD does not look at the things man looks at. Man looks at the outward appearance, but the LORD looks at the heart"* (1 Sam. 16:7).

The Lord does not look at the things that man looks at. While activities of service are great to do and to be involved in, they should just be responses from the heart of a woman who fears the Lord. Otherwise, if we were to be praised only for our works of service, how could that be fair to the bedridden and sick, or others who for a season of life cannot serve God this way? Proverbs 9:10 says *"The fear of the LORD is the beginning of wisdom."* So be wise dear friend. Know that *charm is deceptive and beauty is fleeting but a woman who fears the LORD is to be praised!*

*Father, I praise You, for You are a Mighty, Just, Holy, Loving and Righteous God. Forgive me for the times when I have not feared You as I should but have been flippant in my relationship with You. I do not deserve Your love and gift of salvation – but I praise You and thank You that You forgive me and chose me to serve You. Help me to always have a right view of You and to teach it to my children that they might love You and fear You. In Jesus' name, Amen.*

VERSES FOR FURTHER STUDY

- Deuteronomy 6:13
- Deuteronomy 10:12

- Psalm 19:9
- Proverbs 8:13
- Proverbs 9:10

## QUESTIONS FOR REFLECTION

- How would you define what it means to fear the Lord?
- How does a woman who fears the Lord behave in her relationships? Family? Church? Community?
- Could you be described as a woman who fears the Lord? Why/ why not?